VANCOUVER POETRY

VANCOUVER POETRY

*Edited
and with an Introduction by*
ALLAN SAFARIK

POLESTAR PRESS
WINLAW BC

VANCOUVER POETRY

Published by
Polestar Press RR 1 Winlaw BC V0G 2J0 604 226 7670

Canadian Cataloguing in Publication Data
Main entry under title:
Vancouver poetry
ISBN 0-919591-06-X
1. Vancouver (B.C.) - Poetry. 2. Canadian
poetry (English) - British Columbia - Vancouver
(B.C.)* 3. Canadian poetry (English) - 20th
century.* I. Safarik, Allan, 1948-
PS8295.7.V3V35 1986 C811'.5'080971133 C86-091138-1
PR9195.85.V3V35 1986

Cover illustration: *Once in a Blue Moon* by terra bonnieman.
A silkscreen poster issued to celebrate the tenth anniversary
of the Downtown Eastside Residents' Association.

Vancouver Poetry was designed by Julian Ross and produced by
Polestar Press in Winlaw, BC. Cover lettering by Lou Lynn.
It was printed by Hignell Printers in Winnipeg, March 1986.

This book was published in celebration of Vancouver's Centennial
with the financial assistance of the Vancouver Centennial Commission.
VANCOUVER

◈ CONTENTS ◈

9

Left to right: BLISS CARMAN, SIR CHARLES G.D. ROBERTS, ANNIE CHARLOTTE DALTON, LORNE PIERCE, DR. ERNEST P. FEWSTER (*standing*), A.M. STEPHEN. (1926)

VANCOUVER POETRY

◆ INTRODUCTION ◆

By the definition of one human's life, a hundred years is a long time. In the annals of all the lives through the years that compose the life of a city, one hundred years is a short duration. Vancouver is a young city on the Pacific frontier of the continent. Perhaps no city of its size in North America has equalled it for frenetic literary activity. Vancouver's Centenary seems an appropriate occasion to examine the contributions of the city's poetry community. This volume is an informal social history as well as a literary montage that documents a city that has been particularly nourishing to poetry.

By 1910, the Swiss-born, French to the core poet Blaise Cendrars, traveled across Russia on the Trans-Siberian Railway. Eventually he worked his way by ship to Vancouver and wrote a poem about the harbour before continuing his odyssey across North and South America. Six years later, English-born Dr. Ernest Phillip Fewster organized a meeting in the Rogers Building which became the inauguration of the Vancouver Poetry Society. Its goals were: "1. The study of poetry and criticism; 2. The development of a distinctive Canadian culture capable of appreciating poetry; 3. The encouragement of native talent in Canada; 4. The development of public interest in the work of contemporary poets."

The V.P.S. started out with a handful of members who formed a study group. By 1946, when the society ceased its activities, its membership over the years had numbered nearly one hundred and fifty. The history of the society, the *Book of Days*, lists the then young poets Alfred Purdy and Dorothy Livesay MacNair on its roster. During its early years the

11

V.P.S. was the cornerstone of poetic activity in the city. Meetings every fortnight soon expanded to include readings and receptions. By 1925 the society had published its first chapbook (documented later in this book) and offered a formal "Gala Night" in the Blue Room at the Hotel Vancouver. The guest of honour was none other than the famous Canadian poet, Bliss Carman.

Carman's association with the V.P.S. (he was Honourary President for seven years) continued until his death in 1929. He made numerous journeys across Canada by train and visited his friends in Vancouver even in the last year of his life. Jan Vanderpant, a notable photographer and staunch supporter of the society describes one of the poetry evenings: "Many good friends went through the door always open to them. Remembered is Charles G.D. Roberts [Bliss Carman's cousin and fellow poet] who with pussy-cat on his knee sat as the most contented human being there ever was; Bliss Carman who stood in all his length with the red kerchief around his neck, talking and laughing and we forgetting he was a genius; Florence Randal Livesay [Dorothy Livesay's mother] in all her femininity reading her lovely poems and Ukrainian folk songs."

The legacy of the V.P.S. was its thirty year commitment to give poetry an audience and provide a forum for discussion and social interaction. Several of its members, including Dr. Fewster, Annie Charlotte Dalton, and A.M. Stephen achieved a measure of national distinction by seeing their volumes published in Toronto. It is remarkable to realize, that so early in our city's history, poets traveled across the continent in search of an audience and found it. During the twenties, Vancouver was a hot spot for poetry and it remains so to the present.

The V.P.S. outlived its usefulness by the mid-thirties. The world had changed. Younger poets were involved in politics, and writing had moved away from the drawing room. The V.P.S., like all literary societies, supported a variety of dilettante writers and their associates. Many never broke away from the constraints of Georgian poetry. The value and strength of the society was the unique way poetry was fostered in a new city and the way it insinuated national roots.

In 1936, Dorothy Livesay in her mid-twenties, already a left-winger, arrived in Vancouver. In her attempts to promote the radical magazine *New Frontiers* she met A.M. Stephen, President of the local branch of the League Against War and Fascism. Livesay teamed up with Duncan MacNair (who later became her husband) and organized a writer's group that included William McConnell (who later founded Klanak Press), Barry Mather (newspaper columnist and future C.C.F. Member of Parliament), and Harold Griffin (labour poet). They applied to the Vancouver Parks Board for the use of an abandoned bath house on the beach at English Bay. It became the West End Community Centre, a refuge that lasted as a writer's haven for three years in a city rife with political activity.

In researching this volume I examined many privately printed and eccentrically labelled pamphlets that represented much of the poetry produced in the thirties. It soon became apparent that in many cases while the poet was a confirmed social activist, the poetry remained stilted, unappetizing verse.

A.M. Stephen is the only major figure from the V.P.S. whose work jumped the gap from Victorian poetry to a more open style. Apart from Stephen, Dorothy Livesay, and Anne Marriott, I have included the work of three obscure poets: E. St. C. Muir, Clement Stone, and Burnett A. Ward. Muir's pamphlet (undated), *Poems of Protest*, was handed to me one day by Don Stewart the bookseller. It is a scarce title from his private collection of thirties material.

After the 1930's, I have abandoned strict historical and chronological order to the poems. Joy Kogawa's poem about the evacuation of Japanese Canadians to relief camps was written much later but is certainly evocative of her childhood in the forties. I have placed it next to Kazuko Shiraishi's poem, an even more bitter denouncement of the city of her birth. Shiraishi, born in 1931, went to Japan with her family before the outbreak of war.

13

In the fifties, Phyllis Webb, Marya Fiamengo, and the Burnaby-born Daryl Hine came into prominence. Hine went on to edit *Poetry (Chicago)*. Malcolm Lowry, who would become a novelist of international reputation, wrote poetry in his shack on stilts on the mudflats at Dollarton. Much of Lowry's prolific output remains in manuscript form in the archives at the University of British Columbia.

An anthology of poems about Vancouver could be assembled from the work of Earle Birney. His two volume, *Collected Poems*, contains a great variety of poetic forms written about his chosen city. He taught for many years at U.B.C. and his influence on poetry in this city is enormous. His masterpiece, *"November Walk Near False Creek Mouth"*, is the best known poem written about Vancouver.

The sixties saw an unparalleled explosion in literary activity. Five young poets, including Frank Davey and George Bowering, founded an irreverent little magazine named *Tish*. Their "newsletter", based on American magazines such as Cid Corman's *Origin*, was encouraged by Warren Tallman at U.B.C. who was connected to the San Francisco literary scene. Lionel Kearns, Jamie Reid, Fred Wah, and Red Lane all began publishing their poetry.

John Newlove arrived on his thumb from Regina and moved into the warehouse district under the Burrard Bridge. Al Purdy, Milton Acorn, and Joe Rosenblatt managed the trek to Vancouver from eastern Canada. Each wrote eloquently about this easy city by the sea — a landscape/cityscape that was exploitable, like a new dream. Purdy had been here before but by now was in his full stride as a writer. Gerry Gilbert appeared for the first time in a tiny precious edition entitled *White Lunch*, from Takao Tanabe's Periwinkle Press. Newlove's *Grave Sirs*, one of the finest examples of design and printing in Canadian small press history, was issued from the private press of Robert Reid and Takao Tanabe.

The mimeograph revolution of the early sixties passed mercifully into another stage. Small basement operations turned into full-fledged small presses. Talonbooks, Very Stone House Press, Intermedia, and Sono Nis Press were publishing real trade books of poetry. *The Georgia Straight* was being hawked on street corners and the counterculture was full steam ahead on the streets of the funkiest city in the country.

New poets were appearing in new magazines. Another generation of poets that included Pat Lane, Pat Lowther, Judith Copithorne, and Maxine Gadd was learning its trade. Out of the political activism and the drug culture came the quintessential Vancouver poet. The Halifax-born bill bissett has endured as a survivor and glorious spokesman for the innocent protesting generation of the sixties.

Simon Fraser University, hurriedly built on the isolation of Burnaby Mountain, opened its doors in the mid-sixties. Robin Blaser, Stanley Cooperman and others came from the U.S. to teach in the English Department. J. Michael Yates came from Alaska to teach creative writing at the University of British Columbia. Canadian nationalists were rank with indignation that so many university jobs were occupied by Americans. Vancouver's literary community resembled a collection of scorched cats imitating bad violin music.

In the seventies New Star Books, Press Gang, Blackfish Press, Pulp Press and William Hoffer Books emerged. Names such as Brian Fawcett, Sharon Thesen, Brian Brett, Norm Sibum, Robert Bringhurst, Cathy Ford and Jon Furberg began to appear with frequency. The seventies were the end of a cultural renaissance and the approach of another conservative decade.

Editing an anthology is a dangerous business; somebody is bound to be left out. Another editor might take a totally different approach. My mandate was to put together a book representing the best poetry of Vancouver's young history. I rejected a pretty Centennial commemorative. I passed on the endless poems that glorify the landscape and make it as appealing as a wedding cake. I went for the heart and pulse of the city. Whenever I could I took poems about the human condition in this place of our birth and our choosing.

The poems are approximately chronological, although I have varied the order at times to gather a sense of community.

Red Lane's poem for Milton Acorn is followed by Milton Acorn's homage to Red Lane. Pat Lowther's poem about slugs faces Earle Birney's poem about slugs. And so it goes. George Bowering appears near the end because his recent *Kerrisdale Elegies* is the best writing of his distinguished career. Tim Lander's *Gods* has been reproduced in its entirety. He has been a poet on the streets of Vancouver for twenty years. This is his first appearance in a major anthology. Finally, he takes his rightful place.

I rejected the option of including three lengthy works that would have been greatly reduced by editing: Earle Birney's *The Damnation of Vancouver*; Dorothy Livesay's *Call My People Home*; and Daphne Marlatt's *The Vancouver Poems*. Despite his considerable talent the poetry of J. Michael Yates is rooted ''elsewhere''.

In all cases I have attempted to make the text faithful to the author's intent. The originality of style and spelling in the works of such poets as bill bissett and Jack Spicer is reproduced as correctly as possible. Obvious typos encountered in the originals of some poems have been corrected.

My thanks to Bill Hoffer and Cap Monro of William Hoffer Books in Gastown for access to their considerable collection and for generous support of this project. And to Don Stewart of MacLeod Books. This volume was made possible by a grant from the Vancouver Centennial Commission. My publishers Julian and Ruth Ross gave me the opportunity of turning their idea into this book. Peter Milroy provided eleventh hour assistance. Finally, thanks to Heidi Greco for her valuable insights and her considerable work on the text.

Allan Safarik

Gastown
February, 1986

For my parents: Kathleen and Norman Safarik

FOUND PAEAN TO VANCOUVER
BY RUDYARD KIPLING (1890) *

Earle Birney

A great sleepiness
lies on Vancouver
as compared with an American town:
men don't fly
up and down streets
telling lies
and the spittoons
in the delightfully comfortable hotel
are unused;
the baths are free
and their doors are unlocked. . . .
I thank God for it.
Give me hewn granite. . . and peace. . . .
All that Vancouver wants
is a far earthwork fort
upon a hill —
there are plenty of hills —
a selection of big guns,
a couple of regiments of infantry,
and later a big arsenal. . . .
It is not seemly
to leave unprotected
the head-end
of a big railway;
for though Victoria and Esquimalt,
our naval stations, . . . are very near,
so also is. . . Vladivostock.

*(From Sea to Sea, ch. XXVIII; Complete Works,
Doubleday, vol. 18, pp. 46-47)

DOCUMENTARIES: VIII. VANCOUVER

Blaise Cendrars   *tr. Monique Chefdor*

Ten p.m. has just struck barely heard through the thick fog
    that muffles the docks and the ships in the harbour
The wharfs are deserted and the town is wrapped in sleep
You stroll along a low sandy shore swept by an icy wind
    and the long billows of the Pacific
That lurid spot in the dank darkness is the station of the
    Canadian Grand Trunk
And those bluish patches in the wind are the liners
    bound for the Klondike Japan and the West Indies
It is so dark that I can hardly make out the signs
    in the streets where lugging a heavy suitcase
    I am looking for a cheap hotel

Everyone is on board
The oarsmen are bent on their oars and the heavy craft
    loaded to the brim plows through the high waves
A small hunchback at the helm checks the tiller
    now and then
Adjusting his steering through the fog to the calls
    of a foghorn
We bump against the dark bulk of the ship and on the
    starboard quarter Samoyed dogs are climbing up
Flaxen in the grey-white-yellow
As if fog was being taken in freight

THE LOST LAGOON

Pauline Johnson

It is dusk on the Lost Lagoon,
And we two dreaming the dusk away,
Beneath the drift of a twilight grey,
Beneath the drowse of an ending day,
    And the curve of a golden moon.

It is dark in the Lost Lagoon,
And gone are the depths of haunting blue,
The grouping gulls, and the old canoe,
The singing firs, and the dusk and — you,
    And gone is the golden moon.

O! lure of the Lost Lagoon, —
I dream tonight that my paddle blurs
The purple shade where the seaweed stirs,
I hear the call of the singing firs
    In the hush of the golden moon.

THE LIFTING OF THE MIST

Pauline Johnson

All the long day the vapours played
    At blindfold in the city streets,
Their elfin fingers caught and stayed
    The sunbeams, as they wound their sheets
Into a filmy barricade
    'Twixt earth and where the sunlight beats.

A vagrant band of mischiefs these,
    With wings of grey and cobweb gown;
They live along the edge of seas,
    And creeping out on foot of down,
They chase and frolic, frisk and tease
    At blind man's buff with all the town.

And when at eventide the sun
    Breaks with a glory through their grey,
The vapour-fairies, one by one,
    Outspread their wings and float away
In clouds of colouring, that run
    Wine-like along the rim of day.

Athwart the beauty and the breast
    Of purpling airs they twirl and twist,
Then float away to some far rest,
    Leaving the skies all colour-kiss't —
A glorious and a golden West
    That greets the Lifting of the Mist.

THE INDIAN'S PRAYER

A. Rippon

Oh, why do they seek to destroy the old cabin
   That stood in the shade of the forest for years?
Oh, they with their mansions, their power and their wisdom,
   Oh, have they no eyes for an old Indian's tears?

No beauty they see in my cabin so humble;
   Their gold is their god, they are blind with its glare.
Oh, is there no room in their souls for emotion?
   They turn a deaf ear to an old Indian's prayer.

The laws of the paleface no Indian can fathom,
   His firestick is mighty, his warriors are brave.
Oh, God, hear the prayers of an old Indian woman:
   Oh, let not my shelter be cast to the wave.

Oh, tarry awhile, our days they are numbered;
   The sun god, he beckons his children to come.
The law of the paleface, thou are weighed and found wanting.
   I'm coming, I'm coming, my sun god has won.

So dear to my heart is this home in the forest.
   Its moss covered roof and its ivy clad side.
The eyes of the redman can see in its crudeness
   A picture no artist or poet can describe.

*Aunt Sally's last prayer prior to the expulsion of the Indians from
Stanley Park, Vancouver, B.C.   A.R.*

THE DEAD STOKER

James Morton

He lay upon the barroom floor
   And fought with choking breath,
Then coughed his life out like a tide
   Into the sea of death.

His was no fine, heroic end —
   A biscuit choked his throat —
Through feeble frame and weakened heart
   The cold destroyer smote.

They propped him up against the wall,
   With mild, unseeing eyes,
And face so blue and pinched and small
   And smile of sad surprise.

Tossed like the driftwood, lost and dead,
   Upon Earth's farthest shore.
"A stoker from some ship," they said
   And they knew nothing more.

Yet once he was the darling child
   Of some fond, loving soul,
Who with prophetic eyes and mild
   Foresaw his shining goal.

But fate had cast him far away
   A wanderer of the sea
Blown aimless as the drifting spray —
   Toiling and never free.

His days were passed in stokehole grime
   And sweat from blistering fire
That burned up every thought sublime
   And scorched all high desire.

Yet that fond germ of mother love
   Prophetic in his soul,
Must grow to some new birth above
   Must cleanse and make him whole.

(In a Vancouver barroom, 1906)

THE MORGUE

James Morton

I remember a morgue in Vancouver
   Where, each in the pale silence clad,
They slept in one chamber together
   The good, the indifferent and bad.

And one was found dead in the forest,
   Another was dragged from the sea,
Self-slain by a spirit in torture,
   Now painless and tranquil and free.

And one had breathed death like an incense
   In an aura of saintly flame,
And one had gasped out her hot anguish
   In a hostel of sin and shame.

Yet with all her faults she was human,
   Her failings had died with her breath,
And the face of the angel in woman
   Returned with the angel of death.

And the face of the merciless miser
   Was meek as the face of a child,
While the face of the hard and inhuman
   Was softened and gentle and mild.

Now gone were all lifelong pretences
   Whether piety, powder or paint.
There was peace on the face of the sinner
   And peace on the face of the saint.

They lay there as sisters and brothers
   Asleep from the light of the day,
And the soul of inaudible concord
   Sang from their common clay.

THE VANCOUVER VOLUNTEER

Alice M. Winlow

*When leaving for the front the Vancouver
regiments marched to the playing of "I'm
On My Way To Valcartier," to the tune of
"I'm On My Way To Mandalay." The
sun shone gloriously and the mountains
were never more beautiful.*

I've listened to thy mountain airs,
I've listened to thine Island story,
I've seen the love-light in thine eyes
As thou hast sung thy country's glory.
    I'm on my way to Valcartier,
    I've come to say Good-by.

My heart responded to thy songs
I've thrilled at warlike tales and tender,
O, listen now when I take up
The story of my country's splendor!
    I'm on my way to Valcartier,
    I've come to say Good-by.

O, mountain land where Freedom spreads
Such glorious wings that not a stain
Can rest upon thy snow-crowned hills
Or darken blossoming field or plain!
    I'm on my way to Valcartier,
    I've come to say Good-by.

O, Sleeping Beauty, on thy crest
I've seen the light of sunset shine
As though some Hebe dazed with awe
Had tripped and spilled the crimson wine!
    I'm on my way to Valcartier,
    I've come to say Good-by.

O, Lions, that in mighty strength
Do guard the gates of our fair land,
I've seen thee in the silver light,
The heraldry of twilight, stand!
    I'm on my way to Valcartier,
    I've come to say Good-by.

O, Capilano, crystal stream,
The dew from heaven for our need,
The blue-bird folowing thy flood,
In uncaged flight is of our breed.
    I'm on my way to Valcartier,
    I've come to say Good-by.

O, mountains that the noon-tide sun
Doth burn against the azure dome,
Thy beauty shall my spirit see,
My soul be with my mountain home!
    I'm on my way to Valcartier,
    I've come to say Good-by.

VANCOUVER

Bliss Carman

Where the long steel roads run out and stop,
And the panting engines come to rest,
Where the streets go down to the arms of the sea,
Stands the metropolis of the West.

There the adventurous ships come in
With spices and silks of the East in hold,
And coastwise liners liners down from the North
With cargoes of furs and gold.

Traders up from the coral isles
With tales of those lotus-eating lands,
And smiling men from the Orient
With idols of jade in their hands.

Yellow and red and white and brown,
With stories in many an outland tongue,
They mingle and jest in her welcoming streets
As they did when Troy was young.

The sceptre passes and glory fades,
Only the things of the heart stand sure.
Fame and fortune are blown away,
Friendship and love endure.

Here is friendship steady of hand,
Loving-kindness fearless and free —
Men and women who understand,
And romance as old as the sea.

Tyre and Sidon, where are they?
Where is the trade of Carthage now?
Here is Vancouver on English Bay,
With tomorrow's light on her brow!

V. P. S.
CHAPBOOK

Number One

The Vancouver Poetry Society chapbook: 1925
Ernest P. Fewster, A. M. Stephen, H. Bromley Coleman

THE SPAN

Ernest P. Fewster

Life dashed my eyes with sunshine,
My face with dew;
My ears were glad with the song
    of birds,
And through and through
Glittered the golden morning.
        My slumber broke
        I woke.

Love touched my life with dreaming,
    My heart with fire;
My lips drank deep of his fragrant wine,
    His great desire.
Creation flashed on my spirit —
        My kingdom gained
        I reigned.

Years smote my heart with winter,
　My nerves with rust;
They touched my ears with silence,
　My wine with must.
Death prest to my lips the poppy-head;
　　Tasting I wept
　　And slept.

ON THE HEIGHTS

A. M. Stephen

Wind of forthgoing,
　Breath of the sea,
Lone on the headlands,
　Wander with me.

Voices are calling,
　Low on the sands,
Roses are blowing,
　Wan in white hands.

Lips, in remembrance,
　Lure me to sleep.
Phantoms of faces
　Gleam on the deep.

Love that would linger,
Twilight is grey.
Leave me my cliff-top,
Golden with day.

Wind of forthgoing,
Breath of the sea,
Lone on the headlands.
Wander with me.

ONE MORNING

H. Bromley Coleman

I remember — one hour
On the brink of morning,
I saw a woman
Swaying toward a tenement
Drunken with despair;

I saw a man
Whose eyes were harbours
Of hate and hunger;
I saw a little child
Searching the garbage
Like an eager sparrow;

I saw daffodils
On a market wagon
Swaying in the breeze,
While the clean breath of ocean
Swept along the street
As a clear benizon.

Then I remember
A miracle of dawn —
That touched the hair of the woman
With madonna gold,
That lent to the man
The mystery of Lucifer,
That surrounded the little child
With a garment of splendor . . .

The yellow daffodils were not so beautiful
As these bruised human flowers.

Kahgahgee, the Raven.

The first Vancouver Poetry Society chapbook, 1925 (the only edition to appear in an aborted series) was printed on the private press of Charles Bradbury at ''The Sign of the Raven.'' The cuts were by Janet Eaves.

''A Book of Days,'' a chronicle of The Vancouver Poetry Society published in 1946 documents V. P. S. as the first poetry society to be formed in Canada and the first society to put out a chapbook. A tradition of the Society, later recorded in print by A. M. Stephen, is that ''Dr. Lorne Pierce caught the idea of printing chapbooks while on a visit to Vancouver; he saw the possibility embodied in this first Canadian chapbook, and the Ryerson chapbook series, now numbering well over a hundred, was the result.''

THE EAR TRUMPET

Annie C. Dalton

Edith Sitwell
made a solo
of her auntie,
her rich auntie
and her trumpet,
such a trumpet
as old ladies
give to stranger-
folk to blow in.

Down the trumpet
scornful Edith
sang and chortled
her fine solo
of the Judgment-
day, and crack of
DOOM. . . .

Auntie prattled
of her boy-scouts,
Edith roaring
of the Judgment-
day, still roaring
down the trumpet —

Some day Edith,
too, may need one.
How she'll shiver
when she knows it,
thinking of that
scornful solo,
thinking of the
Day of Judgment;
of the solo,
of her laughter;
of her laughter
and the trumpet;
of HER dreadful,
dreadful trumpet
and the crashing
Trump of Doom!

Foolish, foolish
Edith Sitwell
sang a solo
of her auntie,
her rich auntie
and her trumpet,
such a trumpet
as old ladies
give to stranger-
folk to blow in.

"The Ear-Trumpet,"
an answer to the poem
"Solo for Ear-Trumpet"
by Edith Sitwell.

VANCOUVER

A. M. Stephen

Who can snare the soul of a city
in a butterfly net of words?
Who can melt steel and concrete
into the flowing matrix of song?
Yet there is a word-symbol,
if it can be found.
There is a sign and a password
in the plastic stuff of mind,
an image behind the veil,
that can reveal the meaning of a city.

Ninevah, Babylon, Rome —
the sound of them is an echo in an empty room,
stirring the dust of dead men's bones.

Vancouver —
the sound of it is a wave,
breaking on the shores of the future.

Tune in.
Try to catch the beat
of the wave on a distant shore.

Come by day,
and rub shoulders with the throng.
Be a lone swimmer in the tides
that meet and swirl through the streets.

Rise with the sun in Vancouver.
Let a Jap bring your hot water, a Chinaman cook your
breakfast, a Greek wait on your table, an Italian black
your boots, an Irishman hand you a cigar, a Russian sell
you a newspaper, a Scotch bobbie tell you the time, a
Danish maid clean your room, a Syrian sell you bananas,
a Swede give you a shave, a Jew sell you a new tie and
some collars, an American ask you for a short cut to a
liquor store, an Englishman tell you he owns the show.

Let these things happen and then —
ask the nearest policeman
to please show you a Canadian.

Rise with the sun in Vancouver.
The canyons, between the steel and concrete,
lead down to vistas of water
shimmering like the wing of a mountain blue-bird
Beyond the tangle of masts and the smoke
from the big steamers,
rise dark green stairways to the everlasting snows.
The grinding clang of the street-cars,
the honk of autos, the rumble of trucks
are punctuated by the shrill sopranos of ferry whistles,
the tenor of tugs, and the throaty bass
of ocean liners.

In the C.P.R. yards, the Imperial Limited
halts, panting after its overland flight.
An eastbound freight creaks and strains,
getting under way, catching its breath
before facing the long mountain grades.
Overhead a hydroplane drones and dips
and glides into the upper air lanes.

Let us leave the human stream
drifting into department stores,
flowing into elevators,
rising and spreading
through the skeletons of skyscrapers.
Let us forget the oil sharks, the real estate boosters,
the bootleggers, the bucket shops, the politicians, the
grafters, the gunmen, the mounties, the unemployed.

Let us go down to the sea.
It has stories to tell.
It may know something of the wave
that breaks on the shore of the future.

We shall loiter about the wharves,
casting an eye
to the eternal hills,
towards the Lions couchant,
unchanging against the changing sky,
towards Capilano and the singing waters
of Melawahna and Tslan Tala.

A row of seagulls, bits of frozen foam,
are thawing upon the roof of a freight shed.
The sun dapples their plumage.
They stir and preen their feathers.
They know about waves.
If salt could make a sound,
it might have the harsh tang of a seagull's cry.

Here the elevators tower,
severely beautiful as the columns of Karnak,
grey pillars of the sky,
proportioned and mated to mountain peaks
whose roots are beneath the sea.
There is a golden voice hidden in the pipes
The song of the prairie lands,
of those who sow and reap,
the undertones of tribulation and toil,
the overtones of triumph and happiness,
Spring winds over the green,
Autumn winds rustling the yellow grain —
all these may tremble and swell
from the steel and concrete,
if a master will but press the pedals.

Let us talk with the ships.
Here is a battered tramp,
loaded to the waterline
with sweet-smelling cedar and fir.
The red sun of Japan droops from her stern.
In the shadow of Fujiyama,

41

these fragrant timbers will slowly decay
to mingle with an alien soil.
When the wave breaks,
their dust may dream
of a gateway and a city by the sea.

Leaning lazily against a pier,
reclines an Empress of the Seven Seas.
She is breathing softly
through her great stacks and ventilators.
Soon her heart will pound against her iron ribs
when she breasts the long rollers
and struggles in the grip of the typhoon.

Oh, we may sit all day
on a pier in the sun,
and ask questions of the ships!

We may ask them about Tyre and Sidon
and the dusky crews that gathered tin.
We may inquire about Queen Dido
and her triremes or about the Roman galleys,
beaked like eagles, that destroyed Carthage.
We may say, ''Where is 'The Golden Hind'?
Where are the treasure ships that never came home?''

Ships are laden with dreams
and memories and old phantoms
that whisper through the rigging
and creep along their decks
after nightfall.
But they cannot tell us about the future.

This is Vancouver.
This is the Terminal City.
This is the Gateway City.
Terminal. . . of what?
Gateway. . . to where?

The day is going.
From the mountains,
let us look again.
A setting sun has flooded the city with crimson,
fired western windows with a thousand torches,
and silently slipped over the rim of the world.

With the coming of night,
Vancouver has donned a garment of stars.
Linked and ribboned and looped
in a coruscating mantle of jewels,
she glitters like the bride of an Oriental king.
From her watchtowers she signals
fiery messages to sea and sky,
to ships in the air
and ships below.

Vancouver — crude and magnificent.
Vancouver — sordid and beautiful.
Vancouver — child and queen, without mind or soul.

Terminal. . . of what?
Gateway. . . to where?

Vancouver. . . the sound of a wave,
            breaking on the shores of the future.

NOON ON WATER STREET

Clement Stone

How springtime happy were those quiet half hours
At noon each day, when, the two presses silent,
Three steps and a door led out to the flat tarred roof!
In sweet sunwarmth on the trackside edge we placed
Our cardboards, cushioning the pebbles violent,
(Walt Whitman there I read) and our lunches ate.
The muffled din of traffic's clamorous haste
Made happier there the quiet, where our gaze
Roved tracks and sheds and ships, and then a waste
Of waves, then all the distant harbor's maze.

To pleasure us trains roared in from the east;
Flaunting a flowing plume of smoke, and slowing
To the station with a hissing snort of regret.
Cars here from Montreal, Winnipeg, Calgary met;
Fruit cars from Florida brought many a feast,
Bananas, oranges, melons, asparagus tips,
Pineapples, coconuts, for Water Street.
(Recall those luscious melons, icy, mellow,
With quiet haste extracted from the car,
And carefully tossed to anxious hands on the roof?
A crisp sweet dream that failed not in the proof!
And green bananas, stored till they were yellow?)
Below us now and then went furtive feet
Of frayed old men, who sought with stealth discreet
Their pittance from litter of emptied cars, and culls
As worthless flung in waste cans brimmed with hulls.

Foreign freighters, far-wandered ships,
Peer over sheds, askance to see
The braggart trains; and wonderingly
Watch the pigeons that unharmed
Preen by the water tank unalarmed.

Like clockwork toys the captain and his mate
Pace and repace their narrow deck; the freight
Creaks in the winch; smoothly a sea gull slips
Down waves of air; the mountains lift our eyes
Past forests and snowy peaks to white cloud skies.

Lapses a quiet lull. . .
In sunny silence a basking moment drifts. . .
A freighter imperceptibly rifts
From the dock and draws astern into midstream;
To a chime of bells and a sea gull's scream
She wakens from her land-born dream,
And, pausing a moment for her seaward plunge,
She steadily surges to ocean ways with ever-increasing lunge—
And ere she's gone, twelve-thirty spells our doom.
We leave the sunny peace, spring tanging air,
For our dim and cluttered dungeon room;
Where presses clamor and gnash, lights glare
To keep at bay the corner-huddled gloom.

Those pungent days of moments tense,
Talk, toil and humorous recompense,
Return so pungently and clearly,
It seems tomorrow we might meet there,
Greet casually, work, nor stop to stare —
As well we might — at each other, wondering queerly.

THE LIONS OF VANCOUVER

Clement Stone

Vancouver's Court House Lions,
Stricken to stone by day,
Stare to their mighty brethren,
Snowy, far away.

But sometimes in the night time,
When passers never see,
Nor pause to look, they reassume
Their ageless liberty.

*　*　*　*

The Lions from the Court House
Came roaring down the street,
I really was embarrassed —
Such animals to meet!

But still I hailed them firmly,
Nor trembled with affright;
Whereat their wrath diminished,
They dwindled on my sight.

We walked along together,
They gambolling in glee,
And many a myth and legend's
Strange lore they told to me.

Quoth one, ''I rove the city,
And prowl by day and night;''
The other said, ''The country
Is fullest of delight.''

One cried, ''My name is Vision,
Futurity I see!''
The other roared, ''I bring to pass
Vast dreams, I am Vitality!''

Like voices heard in dreaming
Their soft roar through me beats:
Of hills with cascades streaming,
Of jungled city streets.

STREET SONG
Burnett A. Ward

My eyes are cold, and brazen are my lips,
My smile is bold, but sometimes longing slips
The leash of circumstance, and wells to greet
On Granville Street, or Robson Street,
The ghosts of yesterday on Pender Street.

The yesters when my maiden scorn decried
The Magdalen, and drew my skirts aside
From her with whom tonight I share the beat
From Georgia Street to Hastings Street,
'Neath Neon moons in fogs of Granville Street.

Short months ago and Hope had power to thrill,
But each curt ''No'' ravished the wasting will;
''We need no help''; but yet a girl must eat
On Homer Street, on Nelson Street,
Must break the bread of shame on Hastings Street.

The end I dream — beneath the wharfing piles
Gold hair agleam, and lips too slack for smiles;
Hands emptied of caresses, dropsied feet —
I dared it once, but youth was sweet;
Life's tang has sweetness still on Water Street!

My weird I dree, but fain would I divine
By whose decree I lay before the swine
Pearls now so lustreless, but once so sweet!
Did God or Man pledge rebel feet
Or traffic husks of love on Pender Street.

OUT OF A JOB

E. St. C. Muir

Have you ever pounded the city streets
  Till your feet were blistered raw?
Asking for work to earn your eats
  From every boss you saw?

When every one you asked said, ''No'',
  In tones that cut like a knife,
And you cursed the system that made it so,
  As you thought of your kids and wife?

Around and about on every hand
  The workers deep in the slime,
While the rich are stepping to beat the band
  And having a hell of a time.

If you ever experienced this my friend,
  You know just what I mean,
And you know there is going to be an end,
  Though it may not yet be seen.

When the country that men have fought for
  Denies them the right to live,
When the masters that you have wrought for
  Withhold what is theirs to give.

When the right is pleading unheeded,
  While the powers that be, are dumb,
There is no more parley needed,
  The time to act has come.

THE RELIEF CASE

E. St. C. Muir

I have slept in your lousy flop-joints,
   I have eaten your greasy stew.
I have told the chief, my tale of grief,
   'Twas all that I could do.

I am one of the many thousands
   That are tossed in the great abyss,
Like drift that rides on the flowing tides
   I have drifted down on this.

I have heard the boss's answer
   When I asked him for a place,
And I kept right on, till my strength was gone,
   And the Wolf looked in my face.

Then I shambled down to the "office,"
   Where the hand-outs grow on trees,
Where the big fat chief doles out relief
   And takes your pedigrees.

And you come away embittered,
   Degraded, and feeling sad.
You feel like a bum, as you take their crumb,
   And you've given the last you had.

You have given your all, your self-respect,
   For a morsel to fill your guts,
And your weary feet on the city street,
   Plod on in the same old ruts.

WOODYARDS IN THE RAIN

Anne Marriott

The smell of woodyards in the rain is strong
like six-foot lumberjacks with hairy chests
and thick axe-leathered hands.
The scent is raw, it slices through
pale drizzle and thin mist
biting the sense.
I like to watch piled wetness dripping off
the yellow-brown stacked shingles, while behind
the smoke churns up in black revolving towers
from lean mill chimneys.
Now the broad-hipped tugs
sniff through the squall and swing the oblong booms
by tar-stained wharves,
as with a last fierce gesture rain
smallpocks the oil-green water with a hurled
ten million wire nails.

1936

AT ENGLISH BAY: DECEMBER, 1937

Dorothy Livesay

By the winter-stripped willows in the Park I walked
Gold-washed fountains in the sudden sun;
Brisk the air, white-capped the mountains,
Close at my feet the rim of the land's end —
Everything held in a silent axis, carved in sunlight
Except for the ocean pounding below me, relentless reminder:
Thoughts in my mind clear as heaven's azure
Till the heave, the roar of encroaching armies
Broke on my heart's shore.

Water that has washed the coasts of China,
Shanghai's city, yellow Yangtse;
Water that has cleansed the bloodied hands
And healed the wounds
Signed the death-warrant on too tell-tale lips
Sent to oblivion the iron ships;
Water forever restless, forever in struggle

As a man feels in himself his fevered spirit
Rising and falling, urging and being spent
Into new deeps and further continents —
Until he begins to move with others
Seizing the willows as banners —
Gold-washed fountains in the sudden sun!

DEEP COVE: VANCOUVER

Dorothy Livesay

And still we dream, coiled in a mountain crevice
And still we let the sun
Shift on flesh and bone his subtle fingers
Before his day is run.

Comrade, the thrush will never give us warning:
His singing will not cease —
The bees will hum all down the darkest morning
Inveigling us to peace;

The mountains, yearning forward into silence
Have done with shaking; for the stir
Of centuries is only a brief wrinkle
Where the thunders were.

But we, who love to lie here hushed, immobile,
Whistling a low bird note
Can have no rest from clash of arms behind us
And thunder at the throat.

Here though we lie like lizards on a rock-ledge
Suckling the sun's breast —
Manhood and growth are on us; rise up, Comrade!
It is death to rest.

CHRIST WALKS IN THIS
INFERNAL DISTRICT TOO

Malcolm Lowry

Beneath the Malebolge lies Hastings Street,
The province of the pimp upon his beat,
Where each in his little world of drugs or crime
Moves helplessly or, hopeful, begs a dime
Wherewith to purchase half a pint of piss —
Although he will be cheated, even in this.
I hope, although I doubt it, God knows
This place where chancres blossom like the rose,
For on each face is such a hard despair
That nothing like a grief could enter there.
And on this scene from all excuse exempt
The mountains gaze in absolute contempt,
Yet this is also Canada, my friend,
Yours to absolve of ruin, or make an end.

TALE *for Malcolm Lowry*

Dorothy Livesay

It was not the lock that disturbed — for I had the key
But over the lock, that web of filigree
And the large black witch who watched
From her wheel house, so intricately latched.

Some might have taken warning, gone away
Up sodden path, through evergreen
Past devil's club and spleen
Dashed into daylight and the hard highway

But I took the key, fitted it into lock
And turned. The spider house split loose,
Witch scuttled off to hide, fell prey
For the intruder's foot, the stranger's way.

So did I come to own that hen-legged house,
And the house, surprised, grew meeker than a
      mouse.

*Malcolm, I wrote some poems here for you
Defying all black magic: hear me, hold me true.*

THE GLAUCOUS-WINGED GULL

Malcolm Lowry

The hook-nosed angel that walks like a sailor,
Pure scavenger of the empyrean,
Hunter of edible stars, and sage
Catsbane and defiler of the porch,
Dead sailor, finial, and image
Of freedom in morning blue, and strange torch
At twilight, stranger world of love,
Old haunter of the Mauretania,
Snowblinded once, I saved. And hove
Out of the rainbarrel, back at heaven —
A memory stronger than childhood's even
Or freighters rolling to Roumania.

NOCTURNE IN BURRARD INLET

Malcolm Lowry

Church bells are chiming on the rail
And wheels the frightful killer whale
The gulls are baaing in the creek
And night is whetting up its beak. . .

WHAT DO I REMEMBER OF THE EVACUATION?

Joy Kogawa

What do I remember of the evacuation?
I remember my father telling Tim and me
About the mountains and the train
And the excitement of going on a trip.
What do I remember of the evacuation?
I remember my mother wrapping
A blanket around me and my
Pretending to fall asleep so she would be happy
Though I was so excited I couldn't sleep
(I hear there were people herded
Into the Hastings Park like cattle.
Families were made to move in two hours
Abandoning everything, leaving pets
And possessions at gun point.
I hear families were broken up
Men were forced to work. I heard
It whispered late at night
That there was suffering) and
I missed my dolls.
What do I remember of the evacuation?
I remember Miss Foster and Miss Tucker
Who still live in Vancouver
And who did what they could
And loved the children and who gave me
A puzzle to play with on the train.
And I remember the mountains and I was
Six years old and I swear I saw a giant
Gulliver of Gulliver's Travels scanning the horizon
And when I told my mother she believed it too
And I remember how careful my parents were
Not to bruise us with bitterness

And I remember the puzzle of Lorraine Life
Who said ''Don't insult me'' when I
Proudly wrote my name in Japanese
And Tim flew the Union Jack
When the war was over but Lorraine
And her friends spat on us anyway
And I prayed to the God who loves
All the children in his sight
That I might be white.

I FIRE AT THE FACE
OF THE COUNTRY WHERE I WAS BORN

Kazuko Shiraishi   *translated by Ikuko Atsumi and John Folt*

I fire at the face
Of the country where I was born,
At the glazed forehead,
At the sea birds perched,
On that forehead —
Vancouver, beautiful city,
I shoot you because I love you.
Gasoline city, neither one thing nor another.
Neither
A prisoners' ward — without bars,
Nor the loneliness excreted
By lonely youth,
I wish it could be
a liberation ward,
a liberation ward, where petals of free thighs dance in the sky,
a freedom ward,
a happiness ward,
a goddamn it ward,
a goddamn it divine ward,
a profanation ward,
a devil's marriage ward,
a rich diet ward,
a senior citizen's lasciviousness ward,
a wanton woman ward,
a handsome boy ward,
a homosexual ward,
a wanderer's ward.
In the morning of this beautiful city,
With beautiful Lion Head Mountain
Covered with snow,
In the deep blue sky that soaks
Into the back of my eyes,
I find myself washing my face and teeth
In front of the wash bowl.
It's so sanitary —
A toothbrush and toothpaste kind of purity.

There is not a single bacterium in this country.
Not even that little tiny bacterium
Which the Devil called the soul can grow.
It doesn't exist.
All of them,
The King named Old Morality,
The people in power,
Who clothed the honest citizen
And named him Unseen Conservative,
Who stands at the bus stops —
One of them is a platinum blonde girl
Two of them are old women on pensions.
But nobody knows that the story
Of the beautiful girl who sleeps in the forest
Is about Vancouver.
No one knows that this beautiful city
Is the model for that beauty.
Victoria Vancouver, a girl,
A beautiful girl slowly coming towards me
Who opens her eyes but stays asleep
And comes to me smiling
A diplomatic smile.
I aim at the face of this country
Where I was born, and at the seabirds
Perched on the sleepwalker's forehead.
And then,
As the waves splash, moment by moment,
I stand ready to fire
With the pistol of confession.

PACIFIC DOOR

Earle Birney

Through or over the deathless feud
of the cobra sea and the mongoose wind
you must fare to reach us
Through hiss and throttle come
by a limbo of motion humbled
under cliffs of cloud
and over the shark's blue home
Across the undulations of this slate
long pain and sweating courage chalked
such names as glimmer yet
Drake's crewmen scribbled here their paradise
and dying Bering lost in fog
turned north to mark us off from Asia still
Here cool Cook traced in sudden blood his final bay
and scurvied traders trailed the wakes of yesterday
until the otter rocks were bare
and all the tribal feathers plucked
Here Spaniards and Vancouver's boatmen scrawled
the problem that is ours and yours
that there is no clear Strait of Anian
to lead us easy back to Europe
that men are isled in ocean or in ice
and only joined by long endeavour to be joined
Come then on the waves of desire that well forever
and think no more than you must
of the simple unhuman truth of this emptiness
that down deep below the lowest pulsing of primal cell
tar-dark and still
lie the bleak and forever capacious tombs of the sea

Dollarton 1947

AS BIRDS IN THEIR MUTE PERISHABILITY

Marya Fiamengo

Because they are old we cherish them,
For what we were and are and are to be
Is now the tissue of their being.

My friends I can no longer hear upon the beach,
Their voices come like cavern sounds,
A liquid whorl of lostness as when ducks
Make suctions when they seek the sea,
And nothing young is seen
Except the leaf upon the tree, the loons
       in their seasonal waterings.

I am left to dream my starfish to the wood,
My tree upon the sea,
To cherish with my wrists the bones that will be old,
The bones of my paternity.

Dead wood and wanting of the flesh
And this caress of pebbles on the shore
Waiting the moist embracing of the sea,
Not these nor any sweep of heart
Can plead the leaf back to the pulseless tree
Nor wake the voiceless bird asleep
       in her mute perishability.

Only the funnel of the heart keeps
While yet the pulse beats
That voicelessness complete
When walking in the street:
You feel the wood and hear the loon
       and see the winter welcoming.

NOVEMBER WALK NEAR FALSE CREEK MOUTH

Earle Birney

I

The time is the last of warmth
and the fading of brightness
  before the final flash and the night

I walk as the earth turns
from its burning father
here on this lowest edge of mortal city
where windows flare on faded flats
and the barren end of the ancient English
  who tippled mead in Alfred's hall
  and took tiffin in lost Lahore
drink now their fouroclock chainstore tea
sighing like old pines as the wind turns

The beat is the small   slap   slapping
of the tide sloping   slipping
its long soft fingers into the tense
joints of the trapped seawall

More ones than twos on the beaches today
strolling   or stranded as nations
woolly mermaids   dazed on beachlogs
a kept dog   sniffing   leading his woman
Seldom the lovers   seldom as reason
They will twine indoors from now to May
or ever to never   except the lovers
of what is not city   the refugees
  from the slow volcano
  the cratered rumbling   sirening vents
  the ashen air   the barren spilling
  compulsive rearing of glassy cliff
  from city
they come to the last innocent warmth
and the fading
before the unimaginable brightness

II

The theme lies in the layers
made and unmade by the nudging   lurching
spiralling down from nothing

down through the common explosion of time
through the chaos of suns
to the high seas of the spinning air
where the shelves form   and re-form down
through cirrus to clouds on cracking peaks
to the terraced woods and the shapeless town
and its dying shapers

The act is the sliding out
to the shifting rotting
folds of the sands that lip
slipping to reefs and sinking cliffs
that ladder down to the ocean's abyss
and farther down through a thousand seas
of the mantling rock
to the dense unbeating black unapproachable
heart of this world

Lanknosed lady sits on a seawall
not alone   she sits with an older book
Who is it?   Shakespeare   Sophocles   Simenon?
They are tranced as sinners unafraid
in the common gaze to pursue
under hard covers their private quaint barren
affair   though today there is no unbusy body
but me to throw them a public look

not this wrinkled triad of tourists
strayed off the trail from the rank zoo
peering away from irrelevant sea
seeking a starred sign for the bus-stop

They dangle plastic totems   a kewpie
a Hong Kong puzzle for somebody's child
who waits to be worshipped
back on the prairie farm

No nor the two manlings
all muscles and snorkels and need to shout
with Canadian voices   Nipponese bodies
racing each other into the chilling waters
last maybe of whatever summer's swimmers

Nor for certain the gamey old gaffer
asleep on the bench like a local Buddha
above them   buttonedup mackinaw
Sally Ann trousers   writing in stillness
his own last book   under the squashed
cock of his hat   with a bawdy plot
she never will follow

A tremor only of all his dream
runs like fear from under the hat
through the burned face to twitch
one broken foot   at the other end
of the bench as I pass

dreaming my own unraveled plots
between eating water and eaten shore
   in this hour of the tired and homing
   retired   dissolving
   in the days of the separate wait
   for the mass dying

and I   having clambered down to the last
shelf of the gasping world of lungs
do not know why I too wait   and stare
before descending the final step
into the clouds of the sea

III

The beat beating is the soft cheek
nudging of the sly shoving almost
immortal ocean at work
on the earth's liquidation

Outward the sun explodes light
like a mild rehearsal of light to come
over the vitreous waters
At this edge of the blast
a young girl sits on a granite bench
so still as if already only
silhouette burned in the stone

Two women pass in a cloud of words
  . . . so I said You're *not*!?
  and she said I *am*!
  I'm one of the Lockeys!
  Not the Lockeys of *Out* garden surely
  I said *Yes* she said but I live
  in Winnipeg now Why for heaven's *sake*
  I said then you *must* know Carl *Thors*on?
  Carl? she said he's my cousin by marriage
  He *is* I said why he's *mine* too! So. . . .

Born from the glare come the freakish forms
of tugs all bows and swollen funnels
straining to harbour in False Creek
and blindly followed by mute scows
  with islets of gravel to thicken the city
  and square bowls of saffron sawdust
  the ground meal of the manstruck forest
or towing shining grids of the trees stricken

At the edge of knowledge the *Prince Apollo*
     (or is it the *Princess Helen?*)
floats in a paperblue fusion of air
gulf   Mykenean islands
and crawls with its freight of flesh
toward the glare and the night waiting
behind the hidden Gate of the Lions

IV

The beat is the slap slip   nudging
as the ledges are made   unmade
by the lurching swaying of all the world
that lies under the spinning air

from the dead centre and the fiery circles
up through the ooze to black liquidities
up to the vast moats
where the doomed whales are swimming
by the weedy walls of sunless Carcassonnes
rising   rising   to the great eels waiting
in salt embrasures   and swirling up
to the twilit roofs that floor the Gulf
up to the crab-scratched sands
of the dappled Banks

into the sunblazed living mud
and the radiant mussels
that armour the rocks

     and I on the path at the high-tide edge
     wandering under the leafless maples
     between the lost salt home
     and the asphalt ledge where carhorns call
     call in the clotting air by a shore
     where shamans never again will sound

with moon-snail conch the ritual plea
to brother salmon or vanished seal
and none ever heard
the horn of Triton or merman

V

The beat is the bob   dip   dipping
in the small waves   of the ducks shoring
and the shored rocks that seem to move
from turning earth or breathing ocean
in the dazzling slant of the cooling sun

Through piled backyards of the sculptor sea
I climb   over discarded hemlock saurians
    Medusae cedar-stumps   muscled horsemen
    Tartars or Crees   sandsunk forever
and past the raw sawed butt
    telltale with brands
of a buccaneered boom-log
    whisked away to a no-question mill

all the swashing topmost reach of the sea
    that is also the deepest
    reach of wrens   the vanishing squirrel
    and the spilling city
the stinking ledge disputed by barnacles
waiting for tiderise to kick in their food
contested by jittery sandfleas
and hovering gulls that are half-sounds only
traced overhead   lone as my half-thoughts
    wheeling too with persistence of hunger
    or floating on scraps of flotsam

VI

Slowly   scarcely sensed   the beat
has been quickening now as the air
from the whitened peaks is falling
faraway sliding   pouring down
through the higher canyons and over
knolls and roofs to a oneway urgent
procession of rhythms

blowing the haze from False Creek's girders
where now I walk as the waves stream
from my feet to the bay to the far shore
where they lap like dreams that never reach

The tree-barbed tip of Point Grey's lance
has failed again to impale the gone sun
Clouds and islands float together
out from the darkening bandsaw of suburbs
and burn like sodium over the sunset waters

Something   is it only the wind?
above a jungle of harbour masts
is playing paperchase with the persons
of starlings   They sift and fall
stall and soar   turning
   as I too turn   with the need to feel
   once more the yielding of moist sand
   and thread the rocks back to the seawall

shadowed and empty now
of booklost ladies or flickering wrens
and beyond to the Boats for Hire
where a thin old Swede clings in his chair
like hope to the last light

eyeing bluely the girls with rackets
padding back from belated tennis
while herring gulls make civic statues
of three posts on the pier
and all his child-bright boats
heave unwanted to winter sleep

Further the shore dips   and the sea   sullen
with sludge from floors of barges   spits
arrogantly over the Harbour Board's wall
and only the brutish prow of something
a troller perhaps   lies longdrowned
on an Ararat of broken clamshells
and the flakings of dead crabs

The shore snouts up again
spilling beachlogs glossy and dry
as sloughed snakeskins
but with sodden immovable hearts
heigh ho the logs that no one wants
and the men that sit on the logs
that no one wants
while the sea repeats what it said
to the first unthinking frogs
and the green wounds of the granite stones

By cold depths and by cliffs
whose shine will pass any moment now
the shore puts an end to my ledge
and I climb past the dried shell
of the children's pool   waiting like faith
for summer   to where the last leaves
of the shore's alders   glistening with salt
have turned the ragged lawns
to a battlefield bright with their bodies

VII

For the time is after the scarring of maples
torn by the fall's first fury of air
on the nearest shelf above brine and sand
where the world of the dry troubling begins

the first days of the vitreous fusing
of deserts   the proud irradiations of air
in the years when men rise
and fall   from the moon's ledge

while the moon sends   as before
the waters swirling up and back
from the bay's world
to this darkening bitten shore

I turn to the terraced road
the cold steps to the bland new block
the human-encrusted reefs
that rise here higher than firs or singing
up to aseptic penthouse hillforts
to antennae above the crosses
pylons marching over the peaks
of mountains without Olympus

Higher than clouds and strata of jetstreams
the air-roads wait the two-way traffic
And beyond?   The desert planets
What else?   a galaxy-full perhaps
of suns and penthouses waiting

But still on the highest shelf of ever
washed by the curve of timeless returnings
lies the unreached unreachable nothing
whose winds wash down to the human shores
and slip   shoving

into each thought nudging my footsteps now
as I turn to my brief night's ledge

in the last of warmth
and the fading of brightness
on the sliding edge of the beating sea

Vancouver 1961/ Ametlla, Spain 1963

BALLAD FOR W. H. AUDEN

George Woodcock

As I walked out one evening,
   Walking down Granville Street,
The fog drained off the mountains
   And the air blew wet with sleet.

And there you walked beside me
   In the desert of my thought,
With your lost ambiguous brilliance
   And the wit time set at naught.

The glass was dark in your mirror.
   You held it. I looked in pain.
In that face turned lunar landscape
   I saw the earth of Spain.

I saw the arid valleys
   Where the quick and the dead still wait,
And I knew why your answer was silence
   And how silence shaped your fate.

I walked down Granville with Spender
   In a different, golden year,
And Spender said: "God and Auden,
   They call each other Dear!"

71

O master of my awakening
   Who made me hear aright,
O leader lost of my twenties
   Who elected for faith and flight,

O patient and private poet,
   Who blessed each hovering day
With prayer and vision and practice
   Both God-directed and lay,

And in the American desert
   Kept your Lent and your craft intact,
My mind makes me turn and salute you
   And life as an artifact.

But my eyes look in your mirror,
   I see the rived image it shows,
And my heart speaks out in answer,
   And my desperation grows.

For what the glass has awakened
   Is neither envy nor joy
But the pity I felt at your passing
   By so narrow and wearing a way.

Yet your image speaks like a judgment
   As if your body declared,
"Let me accept the sentence,
   And my brother soul be spared!"

If your Anglican God has received you
   As Auden or Wystan or Dear,
I know that all is accepted
   With irony, without fear,

As the fog drains off the mountains
   And the air blows wet with sleet,
Walking ghostly out one evening,
   Walking down Granville Street.

BARTOK AND THE GERANIUM

Dorothy Livesay

She lifts her green umbrellas
Towards the pane
Seeking her fill of sunlight
Or of rain;
Whatever falls
She has no commentary
Accepts, extends,
Blows out her furbelows,
Her bustling boughs;

And all the while he whirls
Explodes in space,
Never content with this small room:
Not even can he be
Confined to sky
But must speed high and higher still
From galaxy to galaxy,
Wrench from the stars their momentary notes
Steal music from the moon.

She's daylight
He is dark
She's heaven-held breath
He storms and crackles
Spits with hell's own spark.

Yet in this room, this moment now
These together breathe and be:
She, essence of serenity,
He in a mad intensity
Soars beyond sight
Then hurls, lost Lucifer,
From heaven's height.

And when he's done, he's out:
She leans a lip against the glass
And preens herself in light.

POINT GREY
Daryl Hine

Brought up as I was to ask of the weather
Whether it was fair or overcast,
Here, at least, it is a pretty morning,
The first fine day as I am told in months.
I took a path that led down to the beach,
Reflecting as I went on landscape, sex and weather.

I met a welcome wonderful enough
to exorcise the educated ghost
Within me. No, this country is not haunted,
Only the rain makes spectres of the mountains.

There they are, and there somehow is the problem
Not exactly of freedom or of generation
But just of living and the pain it causes.
Sometimes I think the air we breathe is mortal
And dies, trapped, in our unfeeling lungs.

Not too distant the mountains and the morning
Dropped their dim approval on the gesture
With which enthralled I greeted all this grandeur.
Beside the path, half buried in the bracken,
Stood a long-abandoned concrete bunker,
A little temple of lust, its rough walls covered
With religious frieze and votary inscription.

Personally I know no one who doesn't suffer
Some sore of guilt, and mostly bedsores, too,
Those that come from itching where it scratches
And that dangerous sympathy called prurience.
But all about release and absolution
Lie, in the waves that lap the dirty shingle
And the mountains that rise at hand above the rain.
Though I had forgotten that it could be so simple,
A beauty of sorts is nearly always within reach.

BEACHCOMBER

Phyllis Webb

Because she insists on waking nightmares,
I'm thrown out of bed in just the way
old man night is tossed out by day.
What is there left for a faded star?
I escape to the beach at seven-thirty
and alarm the others who arrived before
to stare at the mountains or cry on the shore.

The beach-cleaner combs the left-overs
of burnt-up yesterday's savage sunbathers —
those are eyes that were her pearls —
he rakes his briny treasury —
Heh! Leave something for me!
All he leaves is sand and stone,
but the sea and mountains casually show
Vancouver has a fine enough view
to challenge the world in any part
where illusionist or obsessive goes
to recover from a broken heart.

Is she asleep now? Is the sun poring
over her speech-wisdom, slipping hot money
into her marvellous mouth?
But why should I care if her nightmares flourish?
Here, I am saved — as full of self as the day before —
with pebbles and stones and rocks and mountains.
I'll scoop them up in a swoop for our favourite local
sea-monster, Cadborosaurus (a little off course),
who ferries hallucinations around these waters
and makes our crazed imaginings outroar
the stupid Lions of the North Shore.
Generator of myth! Denigrator of the peace!

I'll stone your horny back clear through
Active Pass to the dotted Gulf Islands
and way into Cadboro Bay where you were first sighted
and from which you should never have strayed.
Not deep-sea monster myth, nor mother's milk,
nor love built our Columbian bones,
but stones, Mr. Cadborosaurus, stones
made this country. This country makes us stones.

POEM

Elizabeth Gourlay

All day long the rain squalled down with punitive force
    driving the window panes
        slashing the deutzia
            shredding its flowers

on the feeding tray the little birds sat
    with their necks drawn in
        and their feathers ruffed

disconsolate too I roamed through the house
    opening cupboards
        and I crushed a small moth
            in my miserable fingers. . .

Later, towards evening, the clouds broke
    and the sun came out
        suddenly
    everything shone
                everything glistened
    even the horns of the snail who made his black way
        to my petunias
            and I restrained my hand
      though I had on my gardening gloves
           and carried my scissors.

MANNA

Elizabeth Gourlay

I should be
indoors
sitting at the telephone
making my duty calls

I should be
upstairs
smoothing the blanket down
upon the bed

I should be
deep in the basement
standing on the cold floor
sorting the laundry out

but I am not
I am floating here
in the white sunshine by the red fuchsia
holding my breath
I am waiting here
for the humming bird to come back

she is all amethyst and emerald
such a long bill
longer than all the rest of her put together
when she dips it in the fuchsia bell

her wings whir like. . .
she drinks like. . .
well, let's say she makes a halo of herself

actually
she should be
over there in the dark fir tree
lining her nest

still
it is imperative
she sip her natural sustenance —

she has to live.

THE ARRIVAL

John Newlove

Having come slowly, hesitantly
at first, as a poem comes,
and then steadily down to the marshy sea-board:

that day I ran along the stone sea-break,
plunging into the Pacific, the sun
just setting, clothed, exuberant, hot,
so happy —
          o sing!
plunging into the ocean, rolled on my back, eyes
full of salt water, hair in eyes,
shoes lost forever at the bottom, noting
as if they were trivia
the wheeling birds of the air
and gulls gorging themselves
on the sea-going garbage
of civilization, the lower mainland,
hauled away by tugs —
                    they,
being too heavy to fly,
and foolish-looking there,
can be knocked off with sticks
from barge into ocean —

and noting the trees whitely flowering,
took off my clothes and calmly bathed.

WHN I FIRST CAME TO VANKOUVR
bill bissett

from halifax by way uv duluth
thousands uv peopul wud swim on
english bay in th sun   now no wun duz
th sewrs go into th watr insted

                    travelling thru wales it
occurrd to me agen wher duz it go from
a train   on to th tracks evree wun sd
my doktor tol me cattul eet shit   thats
what th cows alongside th tracks dew ar
waiting for whn th trains pass

                    so on english bay in th
watrs we cud have cows diving   they
wud b watr cows   peopul wud b abul
to go into th watr agen n cud ride

th cows on th surf n out to th boats
or th universitee

                    i remembr a place in
nova scotia calld cow bay   that must
b wher th cows live

                    iul go back
ther n bring th cows west

DEATH OF A POET *(For Milton Acorn, ultimately)*
Red Lane

It happened that God one day
while walking along the beach
came upon a sponge stranded in a tidal pool.

What are you doing? God asked.

Absorbing life, said the sponge.

Tell me about life, God said.

Squeeze me first, said the sponge.

God reached down and squeezed the sponge.

Sun moon earth sky land sea, said the sponge.

God squeezed the sponge again.

God man woman air ground water, said the sponge.

God squeezed a little harder.

Creator father mother oxygen dirt rain, said the sponge.

God squeezed harder.

All seed womb breath dust tears, said the sponge.

God squeezed with all his might.

Squish, said the sponge.

Is that all? God asked.

That's all, said the sponge.

That's what you think, God said.
Oh.
Well drop around later.
Maybe I'll absorb some more when the tide comes in,
                                         said the sponge.

I've got a date with a sieve, God said.

A sieve? said the sponge.

Have to keep up with the times, God said.
Lucky bastard.
I wish I was a sieve, said the sponge.

You are a sponge, God said.

Yeah yeah.
Those sieves got it made.
Life flows through them all the time, said the sponge.

Life flows through you too, God said.

Yeah.
But only when something comes along and squeezes me,
                                         said the sponge.

Oh? God said.

Yeah.
And I tell you it's pure hell sometimes waiting, said the sponge.

Well that's the way it goes, God said.

Yeah yeah.
I know, said the sponge.

Oh?
Well see you around, God said.

Yeah.
See you.
Lucky bastard, said the sponge.

Just a minute now.
What's with this ''bastard'' bit? God asked.

Oh.
Well.
It's just an expression, said the sponge.

Well I don't like it, God said.

Yeah.
Well.
Well I don't like being a sponge, said the sponge.

Okay sponge.
You asked for it, God said.

And God changed the sponge into a grain of sand
And turned and walked away from the beach.

WORDS SAID SITTING ON A ROCK SITTING ON A SAINT

(In Memoriam: Red Lane)

Milton Acorn

I

He had a way of stopping the light
, making it mark his darkness,
and a depth like a sounding line
played out, swinging its futile
weight far above bottom
, drank all his surfaces.

WARNING... Don't tempt the gods
with too much patience, for he poked
for poems as in the sand for stones
— round firm things, with no entrances

: and would wait for the end
of the time he was in, for
that discovery, the moment of vision
that for him was hard, like a stone

: and I reached out tendrils of thought
towards him... If he told me what a flower
was to him, I'd tell him what a flower
was to me. Thus we worked on each other,
patiently, as if each was immortal.

His dying is like an infinite grey sphere
of nothingness to the left hand of my sun,
and sometimes I draw the nothingness down
to wrap about me, like a cloak with a hood.

II

The saint of stone silences
is dead. The miracle is
that he does not speak,
even as when he made his sparing
moves in our game, his speakings
were flint fragments of no language,
harder silences.

82

The miracle is that the Earth still traces
all the circles of her whirling dance,
and those yo-yos of the sun, the comets
still comb their white curly hair
across the heavens, while he
as in life consents to all their courses.

Doomed to his time, he accepted it
and made a gnomic utterance of it. Caught on it
across, like a bow on a fiddle string
he drew the one note it was meant to say
by his agency, and concluded it
with the quietness that was its continuation.

SPANISH BANKS

Pat Lane

Only drunk and naked are we possible.
If I caress you with my tongue
and me with yours
you're still the virgin bride.
Tongue to tongue we converse
in the same language.

On the road above
carlights curve and touch
for one moment the sea with fingers.
When I leave you
covered finally with sleep
in front of the dust and coals
of our driftwood fire
you'll have lost nothing.

Innocent of survival
you'll slide into shadow
while our child grows
behind your lips
in the wells of your soft cheeks.

HOME-MADE BEER

Al Purdy

I was justly annoyed 10 years ago
in Vancouver: making beer in a crock
under the kitchen table when this
next door youngster playing with my own
kid managed to sit down in it and
emerged with one end malted —
With excessive moderation I yodelled
at him
    "Keep your ass out of my beer!"
    and the little monster fled —
Whereupon my wife appeared from the bathroom
where she had been brooding for days
over the injustice of being a woman and
attacked me with a broom —
With commendable savoir faire I broke
the broom across my knee (it hurt too) and
then she grabbed the breadknife and made
for me with fairly obvious intentions —
I tore open my shirt and told her calmly
with bared breast and a minimum of boredom
    "Go ahead! Strike! Go ahead!"
Icicles dropped from her fiery eyes as she
snarled
    "I wouldn't want to go to jail
        for killing a thing like you!"
I could see at once that she loved me
tho it was cleverly concealed —
For the next few weeks I had to distribute
the meals she prepared among neighbouring
dogs because of the rat poison and
addressed her as Missus Borgia —
That was a long time ago and while
at the time I deplored her lack of
self control I find myself sentimental
about it now for it can never happen again —

Sept. 22, 1964: P.S., I was wrong —

HOW THE WEATHER IS

John Newlove

In Deep Cove they reported rain.
In the District of Coquitlam

the rain has started. In Burnaby
the snow is mixed with rain. But here

there is only snow
and influenza, wet coughing

from room to room in the winter.
I am winning

large imaginary sums of money
at solitaire, shouting:

That's enough, kids!
I want to have a good time.

Or to be good, after
being a fool.

Mixed rain and snow, slush
is out East Hastings way now,

moving closer as the weather
breaks, exchanging

one discomfort for another —
less so. The children

are giggling on a chair together
between fights. What

can it be? We're having
fun daddy just

playing games they say, surrounded
by the world.

POEM ON A FOLDED POSTCARD

Gerry Gilbert

1.
It never did rain
    the day
      ever since you left here. Van
            -couver to Mont-

           real
      Quebec
      there.
it's been hot.

2.
I have been looking
    it is the watching
      not the rest that we look at.
It is.   The watching.
        the resolution
      the definition.

3.
Elsa has
a soft face.

4.
balance: Susan
           is home.
             Jeremy can balance
    the word
        baby.

5.
    I guess love
    moves
        my face
            but apparently nothing is hidden
        in my eyes
          from women.

6.
I quit killing
 time
  I thought

        condem-
            ned I tried
          to stop smoking
 isn't it amusing
  to finish

        a story.

7.
Hot proud people rising
    to the good weather

              on Kitsilano beach.
          when we could clean a space.

8.

      I do not believe
      Montreal
      is round

9.
John: Do not believe
        Vancouver. Love
        Gerry.

BRIDGE POEM (1964)

Maxine Gadd

It troubles me
that i ought
to re
turn
to this
town
as a lover
This
is where my childhood
is
    irrevocable
skin-knowledge, the
foundations of my mind
      this cloistered sky   wet concrete
                the shrouded
possibility of the sea
      compressed mouths   aluminum eyes   tall
        forests that can't
          laugh

And i can't forgive
In my dreams
there are rotting bridges
the many spans
of this water-involuted town
      over the river and the inlet and False
        Creek, the grey entrails
           that empty onto the beaches
             where as a child
                i searched for gold

A poem transcends/through the spoken image from
the sensual to

        the unsayable —
and returns.
At the apex of the grey spans
of my dream
all gaped and gapped,
      the grand black crosses of the understructure

torn,
the only crossing was
    a single, slimey
      plank.
        Below. . .

              the verdigris
And always
i crossed it
on my hands
    and knees

ABOUT BEING A MEMBER OF OUR ARMED FORCES

Al Purdy

Remember the early days of the phony war
when men were zombies and women were CWACs
and they used wooden rifles on the firing range?
Well I was the sort of soldier you couldn't trust
with a wooden rifle
and when they gave me a wooden bayonet
life was fraught with peril for my brave comrades
including the sergeant-instructor
I wasn't exactly a soldier tho
only a humble airman
who kept getting demoted
                  and demoted
                          and demoted
to the point where I finally saluted civilians
And when they trustingly gave me a Sten gun
Vancouver should have trembled in its sleep
for after I fired a whole clip of bullets
at some wild ducks under Burrard Bridge
(on guard duty at midnight)
they didn't fly away for five minutes
trying to decide if there was any danger
Not that the war was funny
I took it and myself quite seriously
the way a squirrel in a treadmill does
too close to tears for tragedy
too far from the banana peel for laughter
and I didn't blame anyone for being there
that wars happened wasn't anybody's fault then
now I think it is

MARGINS XIV
Red Lane

Night
and main street
all around me
lights
making signs to me
reflected
colouring the rain-washed sidewalk
here
I stand
against a wall
beneath an awning
waiting for a black-haired girl
to get off duty
from the cafe
across the street
there
she is
coming out the door
glancing up
turning up her coat collar
she walks away
and around the corner
gone
in the rain
now coming down harder
spattering
splattering reflections
and lights blurred
and her
gone
and I
standing here against a wall
beneath an awning
waiting

Now
just waiting

MILTON & THE SWAN

Joe Rosenblatt

By the dark webs, her nape caught up in his bill...—W.B.Yeats, Leda and the Swan

On a grey September afternoon Milton Acorn and I headed
through Stanley Park on a path shrubbed in on each side by
sixty foot Douglas Fir trees, nakedly green, and thick as bull
elephants in diameter at the base.

We were moving in the general direction of the zoo, almost
empty on a week-day. We would never have imagined visiting
this place on a Sunday because then it is disturbed by tantrums
of emotionally warped children accompanied by pallid adults
who come to amuse themselves at the expense of the Sorrows
incarcerated behind Mondrian bars and shop windows.

So poisonous is the public influx on the preening primates in
their claustrophobic living room that a depressing corruption
unfolds. The Spider Monkeys forget their eloquent dance; no
longer do they imitate Nijinsky, gliding from branch to branch
with fluid ease. No! the ballet freaks are lethargic, deadened.
They are reduced to a state of human sloth, soliciting unshelled
peanuts with tremulous hairy hands. Panhandling street bums!
It is a bleak thing to see the tiny Humunculus cracking open a
crust with thick calloused fingers, teething on tidbits of protein,
then finishing up by pulling himself off into oblivion.

Under a Hansel and Gretel bridge, ducks with pissyellow
eyes were waddling in the brown pond.

Milton was fiercely high on ducks; his face was euphoric: a
tight smile snailed around his mouth. He began to identify each
animal from its collective feathered camaraderie with the
electro-magnetic intensity of a small gerbil running the treads
of a tiny ferris wheel.

He hammered home the facts: descriptions of bird life and
death; bird sociology; mating characteristics and homosexual
hangups of geese; theories on comparative bird and human
intelligence.

'Do birds have pricks?'' I asked.

''No,'' he answered.

''But how then do they do it?''

''They don't do it like we know it,'' he said. ''They just
mate.''

The topic of birds was shattered by a loud declamation against the human condition. It seemed that some degenerate had raped an Emu in the park last summer. The swine was never apprehended. The bird was left to die, feathers and blood, a macabre death.

"Terrible," Milton cried. "Bastards. . . bastards."

"But who would want to rape an Emu?" I inquired.

"People, that's who," he blurted, spitting rage until his face turned turnipy and his cement jaw could no longer support his speech and dropped in exhausted terror. "People. . . that's who. . . bastards. . . ."

My brain pulsated with vivid images of the rape: the bird being violated by some monster tearing her feathers out by the quills and pinning the poor creature on the ground for a brutal entry. . . the bird screaming in excruciating pain. . . blotches of blood. . . the rape artist dismounting and running across the park under a sick moonlight and a caftan of darkness. . . the poor creature so caught up, so mastered by the brute blood of the air. . . .

"Bastards. . . people. . . bastards. . ." Milton's vituperation was ringing in my ears. I wondered who had held the Emu's snaky neck back while the shiteating beast committed his gross act.

"Did you know that the first case of bestiality occurred with Leda and the swan and that. . ."

"Forget it, Milt," I said "I FEEL DEPRESSED."

We pushed over to the seal's pool where brown skinned Colonel Blimps tickled each other through greenish liquid. The water was alive with cigarette butts, spare fish parts, regurgitations and bits of seal excrement. Milton whistled loudly through one of the many gaps in his teeth. A bewhiskered rat's head with cherry black eyes emerged on the surface, wheezed, coughed and spat. "Gosh, they're lovely," said Milton. The seals looked sexy in their oily raincoats, flaked out on the rocks. Some of the water babies were fast asleep and others were just waiting for the attendants to arrive with buckets of fish. At feeding time the seals would suck the fish into their ratty pink mouths, biting at the same moment to keep a firm hold on their meal. If the fish slipped out of the seal's mouth and flopped into the water the blimps would dive to retrieve the corpses. Mealtime brought swarms of screeching gulls who tried to maneuver the fish away from the seals, who in turn barked obscenities while circling the remaining fish portions floating in the pool. I was soon bored with all these hostilities and decided to seek tranquility among the bats. So off I trotted across the park. Milton could barely keep up with me.

"Slow down, damn you," he shouted. I was in the corridor of the aviary when he finally caught up with me. The bird factory was shared by other creepy inhabitants. At the entrance Milton stopped to absorb a green speckled snake vibrating a forked electric tongue. He seemed hypnotized by the Gorgonizing cat cool eyes of the serpent.

"Gosh. . . gosh. . ." he whimpered, and pressed his cigar up to the partition. E.S.P.? There was something deep, mystical going on between them. Inside the glass courtroom the bitch curled up and fell into a deep sleep. I tugged Milton by the shoulder.

"Come one, Milt, let's see the bats." He turned away from the window leaving a fresh residue of volcanic ash on the glass.

"Damn you and your bats," he snarled, and reluctantly followed me over to the bat cage. The image of the serpent was still fresh in his mind. In his enthrallment his cigar had gone out. We gaped at the bats. The black leather umbrellas were hanging by their toes. They were all asleep. Occasionally one would stretch open its wings to reveal a mousey body, a neat set of breasts and babes suckling on each milk shake.

"Did you know that bats ball upside down?"

"No kidding," I replied.

Milton was deadly serious. Any further enquiry would have been a direct affront to his intelligence. I dropped the subject of the copulation habits of bats.

For a moment I imagined I was a flitter-mouse with rodent ears and minitool. I was hanging by my toes from a branch. A hot bitch bat was facing me; I could smell her breath which reeked of fermented insects; she was screeching a thousand pulsations per second; it was a plaintive cry for sex but for some inexplicable reason I couldn't make a connection. What a predicament. ''Help me you bitch,'' I squeaked. Bat's blood was rushing into the dome of my skull. I began to suffer from vertigo. . . a migraine headache. . . a climax. . . one of my toes gave way.

''Gee. . . golly. . . they're cute,'' said Milton.

''I can't get over it,'' I said.

''Can't get over what?'' Milton asked.

''How can they ball upside down?''

Milton's face bloomed a dull metallic sunset. One of the bats was preening itself, brushing its splendid furred belly with a malarial pink moth tongue. ''Gosh, gosh,'' murmured Milton. And while we gawked at the bats, other people trembled past the cage.

''Uggggh. . . look at those dirty bats,'' cried a girl in a mini-skirt.

''Jeezus, they sure give me the creeps,'' cried another.

''I hate them, I hate them,'' screamed a child accompanied by her mother who protectively ushered the brat past the evil eyes of the supernatural. Milton was disturbed by these Christians. His nerves were minnowing under his skin. He was silent as a tombstone. It reminded me of the time he had made a brief but beautiful acquaintance with a killer whale; she was confined to an aquarium only twice her size. Milton harangued the bureaucrats on the parks board, drawing a neat analogy between the whale in her tub and a minnow cramped in a sardine tin. Months later the beast blew her mind; she tried to force an exit through a port hole; her massive head was lacerated by the splintering glass; immediately the pool was drained and the big mother was blasted with tranqs and pain killers and sewn up like a football. However the leviathan was never moved to a larger apartment because only God could raise her up on a fish line. That whale swam in the blood of Milton's heart.

''And then what happened, Milt?'' I asked.

"Why... why... why... she waved her dorsal right back at me; she understood, you know... those whales could be Communists."

Walking back across the park I plumbed my subconscious for a fresh stream of bat poems. We stopped on a bridge. Below, a swan in her wedding gown waddled by. Milton's face lit up under the September sky. He was in love with Leda.

HASTINGS STREET ROOMS

Pat Lane

A wall is two sides. Here
on the inside there is nothing
to hang and I sit looking
at bare spaces around me.

On the outside is another
man. He has painted his walls
in many colours, hung pictures
of his loved ones.
Their screams come through
the plaster like shredded fingers.

A wall is two sides.
I would cut a window
but all that I would add
would be four more walls
and silence
like a painting of tomorrow.

VANCOUVER, I LOVE YOU

Stanley Cooperman

All sorts of
oranges, seeds
of pomegranates shining
like fresh
       moon-juice, heavy
with dancing crabs
looking for tides
in the corners
of your arms, yellow
hair
floating over tree-tops
like seaweed, or
birds. . . .

It's what I like about
the coast, green
things
from Alaska crawling under
the rocks, Russian
sailors
with tassels   and stars
hanging from their
ears,
rolling down Hastings Street
with all their
glands
in their eyes,

and in Horseshoe Bay, the
smell
of oil and salmon,
Japanese dog-
fish lighting paper lanterns
under the pier, trees
poking
blue fingers

through the snow: when
the clouds
fall down from the mountains
there are stripes
of blue space in the fog,

ferry-boats and Englishmen,
and in the park
lawn-bowlers argue
gently
with penguins, who
thump among polar bears and
swans, a serenade
of transplanted bag-pipes
declaring
        war
on rhododendrons. . . .

There's no figuring this
town, anything
can float in with
the logs: used books and
ecstasy majors, Indians,
kosher salami and Danish
pastries: hookers
who wait
for French rolls
in the Italian cafe, where Luigi
imports wives   and cheeses
for Sicilian brick-
layers
with money or dreams
in their pockets.

How did it get here, this
city,
perched like a neon
thumb
on the edge of nothing?
Listen: whatever nightmare
you carry with you
tonight,
whatever tongue you use
to reach your private
taste,
remember that men have built
a magic moustache
under the nose of the Big Snow,
a trick
bigger than all the icicles
on the other side
of despair.

VANCOUVER SPRING: DAWN

John Newlove

City in a cold paranoiac acetylene-light dawn
        slowly warming up
      with gulls in the water
        gulls in the air
           gulls on the buildings
          pigeons and eagles in the air
sparrows and neon in the air
      hawks
        rain and fog in the air
    smell of it
the white-and-
brown-streaked statues of minor men
        or soldiers making european flowers now
          parks and parking lots
gun-hipped policemen
     in brass badges
     blue uniforms
black and
  prowling cars with red lights
        sirens
handcuffs
     and gas waiting to be used
the patina'd statues worn green in the rain
       art galleries and other butcher shops
  heaving concrete sidewalks
and carefully
heaving-breathing
          javex blondes with real wire brassieres
        marking and lifting them
         sailors
  bewildered old ladies
old ladies with strange hats
tall feathers
yanked from the rumps of old odd dead extinct birds
    stuck in them
      stuck in the hats
  librarians and lawyers

longshoremen
      and flowers
      lit buses
   making happy xylophone sounds on their wires
making happy
   xylophone sounds in their full coinboxes
prostitutes with
         their full coinboxes
         busboys
   sharp-cornered banks and evil blindmen tapping on them
with white canes and coins
   cornered customers inside
tourists and whores and flowers
      beer-waiters
         taking taxis to work
            evangelists
   newspaper boxes
crippled newspapermen
slobbering on headlines
         hunchback newspapermen in red wool
   toques and torn scarves against the wind and rain
      university students
         adversity students
         traffic lights
         salesmen
         cabbies

dozens of languages and thousands of tongues
         to twist them
   mouths to lip them —

            standing in the light
            here
            things come —

birds: gulls: neon: police
            rain
         signs in the air.

FRIDAY AT THE EX

Lionel Kearns

His beard
knotted
in a make-shift
loin-cloth

His arms
around a sagging
cardboard box
half-filled
with cake-mix samples
and raffle-slips
from hearing-aid firms

He stumbles
over empty bottles
apple-cores
and crumpled
program leaves —

An escapee
from the Shrine Circus

As the Whip cracks
the Zoomo-Plane
takes people up
and the Snake gives them
six minute thrills
he whispers:

''This midway
isn't licensed for wine
but they can spin candy
out of flesh''

And goes on
tossing hoops
at kewpie dolls
and panda bears

Now he crosses
his legs
in full lotus

Just behind
the Crown & Anchor stand

Where agents display
thirty brands
of silver-base
deodorant

And pitchmen
ramble in their stalls
about a fountain-pen
that writes on walls

But the crowd
from the Fun-House
kick him and jeer

Though the star contortionist
(having always been good
at guessing weight)
pivots on one
pointed breast

And wipes
her eyes
with her tattooed
heels

While the sky
streaks red
above the row
of floodlights

And they jostle him
up the hill towards
the three ferris wheels

SEVEN POEMS FOR THE VANCOUVER FESTIVAL

Jack Spicer

1

Start with a baseball diamond high
In the Runcible Mountain wilderness. Blocked everywhere by
    stubborn lumber. Where even the ocean cannot reach its
    coastline for the lumber of islands or the river its mouth.
A perfect diamond with a right field, center field, left field of
    felled logs spreading vaguely outward. Four sides each
Facet of the diamond.
We shall build our city backwards from each baseline
    extending like a square ray from each distance — you from
    the first-base line, you from behind the second baseman,
    you from behind short stop, you from the third-baseline.
We shall clear the trees back, the lumber of our pasts and
    futures back, because we are on a diamond, because it is our
    diamond
Pushed forward from.
And our city shall stand as the lumber rots and Runcible
    Mountain crumbles, and the ocean, eating all of islands,
    comes to meet us.

2

The Frazier River was discovered by mistake it being thought
    to have been, like all British Columbia,
Further south than it was.
You are going south looking for a drinking fountain
I am going north looking for the source of the chill in my bones
The three main residential streets of Los Angeles were once
    called Faith, Hope, and Charity. They changed Faith to
    Flower and Charity to Grand but left Hope. You can
    sometimes see it still in the shimmering smog of
    unwillingness Figueroa
Was named after a grasshopper.

You are going south looking for a drinking fountain
I am going north looking for the source of the chill in my bones
Our hearts, hanging below like balls, as they brush each other
    in our separate journeys
Protest for a moment the idiocy of age and direction.
You are going south looking for a drinking fountain
I am going north looking for the source of the chill in my bones

3

Nothing but the last sun falling in the last oily water by the
    docks
They fed the lambs sugar all winter
Nothing but that. The last sun falling in the last oily water by
    the docks

4

Wit is the only barrier between ourselves and them.
"Fifty four forty or fight," we say holding a gun-barrell in our
    teeth.
There is still a landscape I live on. Trees
Growing where trees shouldn't be. No trees growing where
    trees are. A mess
Of nature. Inconvenient
To the pigs and groins and cows
Of all these settlers.
Settling itself down
In a dirt solution
In the testube
The water still not alive

5

The Beatles, devoid of form and color, but full of images play
    outside in the living room.
Vancouver parties. Too late
Too late
For a nice exit.
Old Simon Fraser, who was called Frazier in an earlier poem
Played with it
Pretended not to discover a poem.
The boats really do go to China
If one can discover what harbor
Far, far from any thought of harbor
Seagoing, grainy.

6

Giving the message like a seagull scwaking about a dead piece
    of bait
Out there on the pier — it's been there for hours — the cats and
    the seagull fight over it.
The seagull with only one leg, remote
From identification. Anyway
They're only catching shiners.
The Chinamen out there on the pier, the kids in blue jeans, the
    occasional old-age pensioner.
The gull alone there on the pier, the one leg
The individual
Moment of truth that it cost him.
Dead bait.

7

It then becomes a matter of not
Only not knowing but not feeling. Can
A place in the wilderness become utterly buggered up with logs?
   A question
Of love.
They
Came out of the mountains and they come in by ship
And Victoria fights New Westminster. And
They're all at the same game. Trapped
By mountains and ocean. Only
Awash on themselves. The seabirds
Do not do their bidding or the mountain birds. There is
No end to the islands. Diefenbaker
addresses us with a parched face. He
Is, if anything, what
Earthquakes will bring us. Love
Of this our land, turning.

GETTING THINGS IN PERSPECTIVE

Judith Copithorne

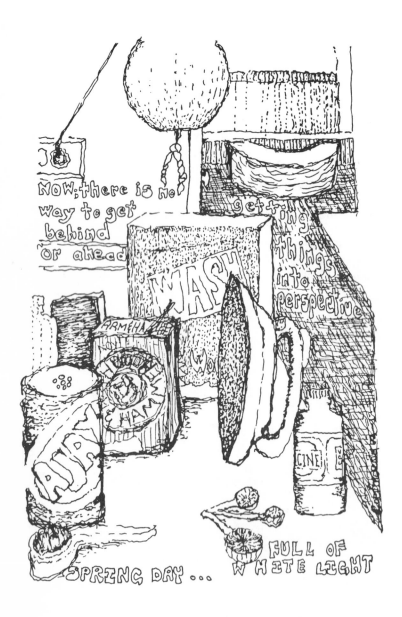

TIME TO BEGIN

Judith Copithorne

Time to begin again. That these things: bicycle,
plant, chair, gentle cat, symbols of inner goal,
supply their own light. Omens of wind, cold
spring bite, knowledge that nothing lasts.

Stop:
move into
being time:
before it's too late
Dreams die:
Shattered by day.
Pray for that art
which may grow
again from
shattered parts.
Sun coming in from
south-west: future
a chasm, past dreams
gone, this present best.

BROWN VELVET
Beth Jankola

Want a cup of hot chocolate/sure do/I'm so
damn cold/not many sellers here this winters
day/not many buyers either/sold the six pale
pink long stemmed crystal wine goblets/what
do you mean/gave them away is more like it/
they felt fragile and ice cold as I wrapped
each one in its separate square of torn news
paper/now this slim greying aristocratic
looking man is fingering my brown velvet/a
beautiful piece of material held up in his
arms to the winter light/they always say
what is a woman like you doing in a place
like this/I say one of two things/oh I'm
called The Jewelry Lady/of I say/oh I'm a
poet/I'd seen him before during the summer/
always with a very old woman/she's a real
antique collector they'd say/but retired
lives in a hotel in the West End/she can't
resist coming out here on a hot summers
day/likes beautiful things/sold her store
years ago/if she likes something she'll pay
money for it/lots of money/she's rich/yeah
he wants the brown velvet I can tell/he
also wants to take me out to dinner at some
native restaurant/the Muckamuck/can Tim come
too and the other poets after the reading
Sunday night/sure he says/look he's not
haggling over the price of the brown velvet/
I imagine/he wants to use it for a throw
over his single bed in that hotel where
the old lady lives/he's bought my velvet/
I looked for him at the reading and after
the reading/I also looked carefully at all
the people in the elevator as we were
leaving/he was not one of them/Tim just
smiled and we all went for coffee and talked
into the next day/at The Swap they said

hotel burned down/the old lady died and
three men residents/that's how much good
your money does ya/yeah they said she's
dead/fried/he's dead too I guess/shrouded
in brown velvet the flames rising.

◆ ◆ ◆

INTERSECTION

Pat Lowther

At Fraser & Marine, slapped
by the wind from
passing traffic

light standards, trolleys
everything has edges
too real to touch

taxis unload at the hotel
the Gulf station fills them up

the lego apartment block
is sharp as salt

And the sunset is tea rose
colour strained, clarified
between navy-blue clouds,
the moon in its first
immaculate crescent

it's an axis
    double intersection
            transparencies

the thumb end
where you press
and the whole universe twirls out
a long seamless skin
a rill of piano music

the calla lily is seamless
yet divided

that cream skin wall
deceives the eye
following round and around
like fingers on ivory

refractions hook under
the eyelashes
you imagine that you can see
honeycombs
                jewels
                    individual cells

texture reveals nothing;

to touch is to bruise

diesel trucks negotiate
left turns,
their long trailers creaking

headlights spurt
at the green signals

it was just here
at this bus stop
I lost my glove
my forty-cent transfer
my book
of unwritten profundities

I tell you they fell upward!
I saw them
      glinting
           catching light
from the thin, solid moon

The Blue Boy Motor Hotel
advertises:
try our comfortably
refurbished rooms
with color TV

the clouds are ink-blue
in the west

mercury lights lie along
the streets' contours
like strings of blue rhinestones

the bus stop bench
is painted blue, it
advertises Sunbeam bread

Don't touch the bench
it could burn you
or crystallize
your molecules with cold

keep your eyes on the sidewalk,
not paved here,
the puddles from recent rain

the Gulf station
could swallow you like a prairie

you could walk into
that phone booth
and step out between the planets

TH EMERGENCY WARD

bill bissett

So as i was regaining con
sciousness alone paralysd th shrink
was skreeming at me that hed never
seen such an obvious case of a
psychologically feignd man
ifestation of an apparently
physiological injury sumone
had phond in or sumthing that
i was a paintr so he sd that
again it was obvious that i was
trying by pretending
paralysis to get out of
painting that damn it

hed make me move again if he
had to shock me into it but
doctor hes bleeding nurse
shut up yu shud know
that advanced catatonia
and bleeding are not in
compatible sorry doctor
th ambulance is getting
ready so they were undr
his ordrs he kept shouting at
me bout yu and yur
kind hel fix us alright

bunduling me off to River
view th out of city mental
hospital extremely undr
staffd for shock treatment
when as they were rollin me
onto th stretchr this
beautiful neurologist chick
staff doctor sz stop thats
an intr cerebral bleed

if i ever saw one so as
th shrink had got me
first they had to
make a deal so this

is my re entry i thot so far out
so th trip was if th neurologist
chick cud get proof of an
inter cerebral bleed then i
wud go to th neurology ward
othrwise th shrinks wud get
me with intr cerebral bleed
shock treatment sure wud kill
me alright iud go out
pretty fast i gess so befor
th operation th neurologists
came to see me askd whethr i
wantid to go ahead with th
trip to th o.r. why not i
sd what have we got to

lose maybe yr life she sd well
lets get on with it alright she sd
do yu want partial total or local
iul take total evry time i sd
playd jimi hendrix water
fall thers nothing to harm yu
at all in time to th blood gushin
out of th ventricals up there to
keep them relaxd 12 neurologists
inside my brain like fantastik
voyage woke up in th middul
of th operation gave em a poetry
reading sure was fun they
put me out again sd i mustuv
known my way round drugs

115

cause they sure gave me a lot
well they got proof of th intr
cerebral bleed thing rescued
me from th shrinks who
still usd to sneak up th back
stairs to get at me but th nurses
usd to kick them back down
those neurologists and th nurses
in that ward sure were good
to me usd to lift th covrs off my
head which was liquifying or sum
thing my eyeballs turning to
mush ask me if there was
very much pain strong tendr
angel eyes iud say theres

so much pain don't worry we'll
bring yu anothr shot thank yu
iud moan and now i can even
write this tho th spastik fine
print in th elbow or wherever
it is is kinda strange but ium
sure lucky and grateful
fr certain that it was an intr
cerebral bleed

MARKETS: II

Judith Copithorne

The Chinese store on the corner has gone, just
went past yesterday and there it was, less
fruit than before but still there and now today,
its gone with only the old cases to remind you
of it, actually it's not much different than it
was before, just a little barer really some
of the color gone, and the old man with the
blue open worked skull cap his wife crocheted
for him, and his big bony wife smiling her
gold tooth smile at you each time you came in. . .
Gradual, it was that change in the quantity and
each thing got older, sat on the shelf for
longer each time. . . Washing soda is something
hard to get and they carried that and bok
choy, washing soda was the only thing I bought
there recently as a matter of fact.

ALCAZAR

John Newlove

I think I've seen you somewhere,
said the girl in the pub, sitting
at the next table. We joined her,
but could not think where
we might have been together.

At the same table, the fat woman
(happy or sad) said, I wish
I was a bird, I'd take my suitcase
in my beak and fly away
to Copenhagen. Copenhagen?

But that girl in the pub: she was plump,
not smart. She sat
with her husband, married
after a 9-day knowledge of him,
English sailor, ship-jumper.

I'm flying to Copenhagen,
the fat woman said; her suitcase
was not in her beak. The girl and I
could not think where we might have been
together. The beer mounted in us.

The fat woman dreamed. The sailor
complained of the beer and cigarettes here;
the girl spoke of her marriage
and husband. It would be alright, she said,
if he wouldn't burn me with cigarettes.

ANNIE OF THE CORRIDORS

Peter Trower

Madonnas of the fogged past
you move through endless passageways
interminable rooms
constant among the transcience
of transient hotels
aging hennaed women with much English
pretty Slavic girls with little
Betty   Olga   Doris   Petruska
and the nervous one with the unpronounceable name.

Lost ladies of morning halls
like displaced mothers   amnesiac sweethearts
triggering vague dreams
of love or guttering lust
in the drifting minds of lonely men.

Annie of the corridors
queen of the Marble Arch chambermaids
how I imagined I loved you
in the pinched and alienated days
when nothing like love seemed likely again.

Annie of the fine roan hair
the full proud man familiar body
the fortyish worldwise sensual face
you ran your troops like a kindly madam
and my fantasies like a succubus.

Annie, my seamstress of dreams
who once sewed two buttons on my one shirt
after a drunken scuffle
who sometimes shared a beer with me
but never my bed.

Annie, immovable Annie
rejecting my clumsy advances
telling me with enormous finality:
"You're young enough to be my son
and you drink too much."

Annie, empress of linen closets
in visions, I stride surely back to you
no longer a boy or drunk   King of the Janitors
with coveralls and an amorous moustache
We are made for each other   we make love
in all the empty rooms
are married by the Manager
and rule that dusky corridor empire forever.

◆ ◆ ◆

ITS RAINING ALL OVR TH CITEE
ITS RAINING

bill bissett

all ovr th citee its raining all ovr th
citee   its raining all ovr th citee   its
raining all ovr th citee   its raining all
ovr th citee   its raining all ovr th poli
tishans   its raining all ovr th citee   its
raining all ovr th citee   its raining all
ovr th hookrs hudduld in church doorways
its raining all ovr th citee   its raining

all ovr th citee   its raining all ovr th
citee   all ovr th mayor   all ovr th soshul
workrs   its raining all ovr th citee   its
raining all ovr th citee   all ovr th priests
all ovr th teechrs   all ovr th poets   its
raining all ovr th citee   all ovr th news
vendors   its raining all ovr th citee   all
ovr th actors   its raining all ovr th citee
its raining all ovr th buildrs   all ovr th
squirrels   its raining all ovr th citee   its
raining all ovr th citee   all ovr th shopprs
its raining on   all ovr th lawyrs   all ovr
th judgus rushing to chambrs ther robes
getting wet   nuns inside fast ther habits
getting wet   puttin my hat on quik my hed
getting wet   its raining all ovr th citee
its raining all ovr th citee   all ovr th
pigyuns   all ovr th bus drivrs   all ovr
th lotteree sellrs   all ovr th umbrella
laydee looking up at th sky   all ovr th
shopping cart peopul   all ovr th spare
change peopul   all ovr th swimming pool
vinyards   all ovr th playgrounds   all ovr
th publishrs   all ovr th citee   all ovr
th aldr peopul   all ovr th doktors   its
raining all ovr th dansrs   th birds   all
ovr th inspektors th playrites th produsrs
th direktors its raining on   all ovr th citee
all ovr th roof top deels   th golf courses
th bridges   its raining all ovr th citee
yu n me cumming togethr agen its raining on
its raining all ovr th citee   its raining
all ovr th citee   its raining all ovr th
citee

121

SLUGS
Pat Lowther

Yellow gray
            boneless things
    like live phlegm
heaving themselves
gracelessly
across sidewalks

laboured
as though the earth
were not their element
oozing their viscid mess
        for godsake don't
                    step
                            there
ugh ugh
horrible pulp

:two of them:
the slime from their bodies
makes a crystal rope
                suspending
them   in air
            under
    the apple tree

    they are twined
            together
in a perfect spiral
    flowing
                around
    each other
            spinning
    gently
            with their motions
Imagine
    making love like that

SLUG IN WOODS

Earle Birney

For eyes he waves greentipped
taut horns of slime   They dipped
hours back   across a reef
a salmonberry leaf
then strained to grope past fin
of spruce   Now eyes suck in
as through the hemlock butts
of his day's ledge there cuts
a vixen chipmunk   Stilled
is he — green mucus chilled
or blotched and soapy stone
pinguid in moss   alone
Hours on   he will resume
his silver scrawl   illume
his palimpsest   emboss
his diver's line across
that waving green illim-
itable seafloor   Slim
young jay his sudden shark
The wrecks he skirts are dark
and fungussed firlogs   whom
spirea sprays emplume
encoral   Dew his shell
while mounting boles foretell
of isles in dappled air
fathoms above his care
Azygous muted life
himself his viscid wife
foodward he noses cold beneath his sea
So spends a summer's jasper century

Crescent Beach, B.C.

THE TOUCH

Gerry Gilbert

Snails everywhere:
On the footpaths
Drowned in the tanks of rotting rain water
In all places —
I meet the shells in my wanderings
My boots are minutely scarred
— On all damp places
Suitable for being stuck to.
Coming and going to and from them
Across our kitchen window
(Unlike crossing a sea for Helen)
On the great stone holding the gate
(Not at all an old Lama in Himalayan vertigo)
Cold snail in his crisp shell
I remember the agility of his eyestalk
And the touch of his weak skin
And his fear of me
May his delicate brethren multiply

MOUNTAINS

Skyros Bruce

the mountains are real
they are me
i slept beside these mountains
near this water
long before i was born
in the cocoon of my mother's
womb.   lain by this river.
once i envisioned a large
bearded head floating in the water
half filling the inlet
i could see it from
the golden arc of the bridge. the lions.
sometimes i stand
for long spaces of time
looking at the mountains
and the sunny water in the distance,
at the land
at the clouds
or i lie on my back
looking up at the immense blueness
enjoying the sky
the earth is soft and curved
under my/your body
and i remember what he said,
when all your friends are gone
you still have this
the mountains   the oceans
and yourself

someday soon before you leave
we will go far away to a cabin
in the trees
and enjoy silence

COAST RANGE

Pat Lowther

Just north of town
the mountains start to talk
back-of-the-head buzz
of high stubbled meadows
minute flowers
moss gravel and clouds

They're not snobs, these mountains,
they don't speak Rosicrucian,
they sputter with
billygoat-bearded creeks
bumsliding down
to splat into the sea

they talk with the casual
tongues of water
rising in trees

They're so humble they'll let you
blast highways through them
baring their iron and granite
sunset-coloured bones
broken for miles

And nights when
clouds foam on a beach
of clear night sky,
those high slopes creak
in companionable sleep

Move through grey green
aurora of rain
to the bare fact:
The land is bare.

Even the curly opaque Pacific
forest, chilling you full awake
with wet branch-slaps,
is somehow bare
stainless as sunlight:

The land is what's left
after the failure
of every kind of metaphor

The plainness of first things
trees
gravel
rocks
naive root atom
of philosophy's first molecule

The mountains reject nothing
but can crack
open your mind
just by being intractably there

Atom: that which can not
be reduced

You can gut them
blast them
to slag
the shapes they've made in the sky
cannot be reduced

THE CRABS UNDER
THE SECOND NARROWS BRIDGE

Brian Brett

The scaffolding of the bridge
collapsed like a tinkertoy,
a folding accordion of men
hurled into shadows against the sun,
flightless birds that were
a gift from the garish sky.

The scavenger crabs,
eyes on stalks
found a new feast
in the cobwebs of the greasy brain,
living on memories of hammers
and lawns that needed mowing.

Then they spit out
little bubbles of blood,
a rising stream
that marked every man's grave.

Now the men inhabit the crabs,
the trace of each face
delicately etched
on the barnacle-crusted shells,
wide eyes looking for the sky.

At night, the orange-red husks
clatter their claws; it's a
secret conversation in code
revealing the real mechanics
behind the construction of crabs.

You can hear them
tapping out their dreams

as the clicking ghosts
build under water
a whispering bridge of claws.

APPARITION ON
THE SECOND NARROWS BRIDGE

Stanley Cooperman

A man walked on the bridge
with a green umbrella,
and his eyebrows
were on fire,
and he looked at my headlights
dancing
(the man with the green
           umbrella)
between drops of grease
falling
from the sky.

In one hand he carried
a dead salmon
sheltered
from the night
by the green umbrella,
and he walked on the bridge
while
clouds
fell into the river
with a poc
       poc poc
like very small
black
    teeth.

Why was he on the bridge?
why did he carry
a green
       umbrella
when the rain
came up from the river
to wet his feet?

why
was he burning
on a bridge in the middle
of the nightmare city, over
a river
filled with policemen
and dead
      fish?

◆ ◆ ◆

THE KNOWLEDGE OF TREES

Michael Bullock

Evolving through countless millennia, great trees contain,
written in the circles of their yearly growth in hieroglyphics
as yet unintelligible to man, profound secrets
concerning the universe. If we could unroll a tree
as one unrolls a carpet, spread it out flat and study it
intensively for several centuries, until we learned
the language of its messages, we should discover facts
in the light of which we could revolutionize life on earth.
Even now this information is still being recorded
and one day, if we leave enough of the largest trees
still standing, people with sufficient wisdom to know
where true wisdom is to be found will unroll trees
and from their scrolls will gain the knowledge we disdain.
Meanwhile, how foolish to cut down trees,
turn them into paper and print on this paper
the idiocies that we consider to be wise.

KILLER WHALE

bill bissett

"...i want to tell you love..."   *Milton Acorn*

we were tryin to get back to Vancouver
again cumming down th sunshine coast, away
speeding from th power intrigue of a
desolate town, Powell River, feudalizd
totally by MacMillan Blowdell, a different
trip than when i was hitch-hiking back
once before with a cat who usd to live
next door to Ringo Starr's grandmother
who still lives in th same Liverpool house
even tho Ringo offerd her a town house
in London, still shops at th same places
moves among th Liverpool streets
with th peopul, like she dusint want
to know, this cat told me

away from th robot stink there,
after th preliminary hearing, martina
and me an th hot sun, arguing
our way thru th raspberry bushes
onto a bus headin for Van, on th ferry
analyzing th hearing and th bust, how
th whole insane trip cuts at our life
giving us suspicions and knowledge
stead of innocence and th bus takes
off without from th bloody B.C.
government ferry — i can't walk too good
with a hole in my ankle and all why
we didn't stay with our friends back
at th farm — destind for more places
changes to go thru can feel th pull
of that heavy in our hearts and in th air,

131

th government workmen can't drive us
20 minutes to catch up with th bus, insane
complications, phoning Loffmark works minister
in Victoria capital if he sz so they will they say
he once wrote a fan letter to me on an
anti-Vietnam pome publishd in Prism, ''. . . with
interest. . .'' he sd he read it, can't get him
on th phone, workmen say yer lucky if th
phone works, o lets dissolve all these phone
booths dotting surrealy our incognito intrigue
North American vast space, only cutting us all
off from each other — more crap with th bus
company, 2 hrs later nother ferry, hitch
ride groovy salesman of plastic bags, may
be weul work together we all laughing say
in th speeding convertibel to Garden City, he
wants to see there th captive killer whales.

Down past th town along th fishing boat dock
th killer whales, like Haida argolite carvings,
th sheen — black glistening, perfect white circuls
on th sides of them, th mother won't feed
th baby, protests her captivity, why did they
cum into this treacherous harbor, th times
without any challenge, for food, no food
out there old timer tells me, and caught,
millions of bait surrounding them, part of
th system, rather be food for th despondent
killer whales than be eat by th fattend ducks
on th shore there old timer tells me, and
if th baby dies no fault of mine th man
hosing him down strappd in a canvas sack
so he won't sink to th bottom, ive been hosing
him down 24 hrs a day since we netted em,

and out further a ways more killer whales
came in to see what was happening and they
got capturd for their concern, th cow howling
, thrashing herself in and out of th water, how
like i felt after getting busted, like as all
felt, yeah, th hosing down man told me, we got
enuff killer whales for 2 maybe 3 museums, course
th baby may die but there's still plenty for those
peopul whos never see animals like these
here lessen they went to a museum.

We went back to the convertibel along th narrow
plank, heard th cow howl sum more, th bull
submerged, th man hosing th listless baby,
th sun's shattering light, them mammals aren't going
to take it lying down we thot, missed another ferry
connection, changd, made it, staggerd
together into town.

BIRNEYLAND

Lionel Kearns

Rising late the first morning
after a good night's sleep
we eat and go down to carry up
water from the spring. Slowly
city poisons rinse
from body and mind. After lunch
walking back from the old cemetery
we lose our way and end up high
on the cliffs over the sea.
Freighters and ferries are dodging
fishboats and sounding their horns
as they enter Active Pass. We
undress and salute the Gulf
the islands, sun, sky, and life
itself that here beside us
snaps dried gorse seed pods
twitches the chattering chipmunk
on a twig, sends a little snake
skittering into the leaves
along the trail. It's hot
so we make love in the shade
and afterwards climb down
to the rocks for a cold swim.
When we get back to the cabin
Earle is still typing busily.
Maya begins to make supper
and I go out on the porch
to collect poems as they come
zinging in on the wind. Later
that evening we talk about
Kootenay Lake and the sternwheelers
we both knew in our boyhood.
The moon comes up and lays down
a silver path across the water
to our feet. It's an old story
but I had almost forgotten

TREE HISTORY
Mona Fertig

For six years the wind has shaken this tree.
Has pulled the leaves their windy dresses off
the snakeskin down. Scissors have fallen from
the branches. Fingers lean and painful. Snipping
and poking at our broken sides our failures. The
days and years have sped by. Rings of wood round
and numbered. Unfolding sand and pearls   gardens
and walls   barbed wire   a typewriter held back
held back. And the mornings and midnights reach
around and under me. Time pushing me slowly gently
along its river route waterway   no turning back
no stopping or getting off   through thunder
rolling and the wounds of love and war. At the
end a Gem a wisdomstone or a full-blown Tree.
The fingers tear under the skin's layers. The
serpent curls up the spinetrunk. When Time passes
like this there are roots to unknot or bury deeper.
Rivers to catch. Tears to flow. Birds strain in
their string nests. The wind the wind gets inside
of me. Wild flowers push up from the base basement.
Between the human edges. Broken glass. The Mirror
you once held. Children and Wishes tumble out of
the trunk like birds or bright ribbons into the sky.
No law of gravity here. The wind sweeping them
as many coloured as light as waves or shells.
As strong as the sun. Bright and different packages.
Dreams gulling. Stories of time running ahead
out of the veins. Time with boats and brave ones.

GODS

Tim Lander

The crazy gods will crown you
with their golden speckled laughter:
they ride their elephants
from the sea
through the dull cities
to the highest mountains;
they come in robes of ivory,
slippers of parrot's feathers
and polished basalt
jockstraps

the insane gods
pilgrimage with purpose
through valleys of honeysuckle
always asking for you
in brothels of linoleum
and markets
of rust and arborite:
their lips, as they come,
are swollen and sticky
with the pustules
of questions

they search among sleepers
in houses
of worn newspaper
in gardens and parkbenches
public beaches
dilapidated trees
and the dusty scrub
on the edge of cities

the adventurous mad deities
are hungry for an eyeful
of your esteemed person:
honourably
they're gonna catch you,
reverently

suck y'r lily white skin,
hug you
so to speak
till you turn slowly
black and blue and yellow
and noises creak
like old fruit trees,
involuntary
from y'r barren mouth

the amorous pathetic gods
are on you
moss growing on their golden thrones,
big trucks have hauled away
their sacred groves
how long ago they lost their love
praise   sacrifice
even worshippers
they do not know

and the hungry gods
are on you
caught like a candy wrapper
between the parking lot
and the bridge rail
caught by the pasted store window
sold out last week
today, full of mutilated posters
they've got you
the hungry gods
by the guns of cambodia
by the black nursing mother
of angola, rifle slung
by the metal worker's hall
and the fisherman's hall
the crazy gods have got you
and they suck you cold in longing

and the great gods
all of them
are coming
to ask you
for all the spare change,
lying to your muddy mind:
you notice them beside you
suddenly drinking beer
with great gulps and burps
and in the bus
with enormous histories
of how they lost
their last two jobs
and what they told the boss
at the end of the shift
when they were found
behind the generator shed
with an empty mickey of rye

and the coffee counter too:
you're sure they're standing behind you
as you slip an extra donut
into your pocket

you've met them
on every corner
mumbling about past glories
fighting their way
through Italy
begging dimes
for a bus journey
to a fabulous location
they'll never get to

and the lost gods
are coming with a question:
a small one
for a cigaret

or a match. . .
coming with wet feet
their heads on fire

and the dilapidated gods
with memories
of perfumed temples
slumber in doorways
nervously watch rainclouds
and examine broken umbrellas
discarded already
by urgent mortals,
possibly fixable
with a piece of bent wire

and the silken gods
out of time with angels now
sing lullabies by sooty trees
sing of the sodden paper
of their past
transparent beauty

and the horrendous singing gods
of wonderful lunacy
are sniffing your footsteps
in the alleys of the city

the awful gods
on old goat feet
and of course
on gossamer wing
are quite desirous
of your grass thin person
to pick your mind
of its fruity imaginings

and the great mad gods
measure their might

descend
in big black boots
down the glistening
rainwashed sidewalk
visiting the cafes
rattling in washrooms
sturdily pouncing
on your embittered brothers

and the fat senile gods
will deliciously gobble you up
roll on your carcass
in parks of dirty trees

Oh the gods! the gods!
you forgot them once:
you thought they didn't count
but they know so well their ABC's
through the yellow pages
of your sentimental mind
Oh the gods! the gods!
can you feel their fingers
tramping down the labyrinths?
you wish, too late,
y'd safely ate the maps

and the crazy gods
are dancing
in that well hidden emptiness
of your defunct imagination

and the dumb gods
are looking
in all the wrong places:
you gave them the slip again
when you jumped on the bus;
they were searching in cafes
you hid among tables

they were queuing for skinflicks
you sat drinking beer
they were off to the races
you swam in the ocean
and the spaced out drunken gods
are tripping round the galaxy
looking for a footprint
of a size eleven boot
that's yours

and the idiotic imbecilic gods
are wandering in snowfields
of a far northern wilderness
of an even colder planet
and the gods are coming home again
in whirlwinds
of honest stars
singing dusty melodies
of clouds of incandescent gas
and the watchman of the heavens
is dreaming out a fantasy
of strawberry shortcake
and soft ice cream

and strange dark gods are zooming
on mythologic motorcycles
making a tour of heaven
in coffeeshops of lunacy
and gardens of disgusting peace

and the crazy gods are on you
masked as cats
and foul old men
and the gods
with yellow spittle
are climbing your carcass
with spiked boots and ice axe:

the prospectors of your sacred body
are reaching to the core of things
polluting y'r spinal fluid
with their stinking cloudy urine

the kind gods
have caught you
hold you in a hammerlock
press your nose to the cobblestones
in an alley of stenches
and they kick in your teeth
in this rain filled paradise
and the honeyed gods
are very fierce
in the pursuit
of your despair

and the insane gods
those little cherubs of crazy
are waiting behind a tree
as you piss against a bush
drinking beer and giggling
surely at the next table
always a spot in memory
rolling and quivering
behind your bloodshot eyes
possessing with much boisterousness
your narrow junkfilled skull

and all those gods
all of them
the whole slimy crew
are jumping down the stairs of heaven
armed with obscenities
and gorgeous temptations,
catch you by the heels
on the smutty concrete
sidewalk

and the gods
you see — you don't?
the recognizable, abstract
distant, deified fellows
each one a little past his prime
the slightly corrupt
but dignified
and sleepy
unaccustomed fathers
of unwelcoming galaxies
out there beyond the potted plants,
windows, and the prevailing weather
the mutterers of history
murderers of adolescent dreams
suspect ladies of the star speckled universe
large hungry slightly slobbering eaters
of the warm flesh of accident victims
and the casualties of private wars
in unpronounceable jungles
under the eye of god alone
the great white bloody creature
the one chairperson of the universe
the gentleman who disposes with glee
your miserable fates in the mud
of the chance unlucky biosphere you inhabit

the crazy gods will crown you
you drinkers in alleys
the crazy gods will crown you
you dancers in streets
the crazy gods will crown you
sleeper on stained mattress
the crazy gods. . .
petty thief   scrounger   bagman   nosepicker
. . . with their golden speckled laughter!
*blasphemous lumpen prole,   arselicking
coffee drinker*

the golden gods. . . *welfare bum,*   *no good*
remittance man   stranger   stranger
. . . will mock you. . . *father of brats*
father of lovely fat greedy babies
. . . with their crazy gilded laughter
screwer   unfaithful
the purple gods. . . *word monger   hypocrite*
. . . will bite you. . .
nose mouth
and prick
ribs skin and nipples
. . . with their golden. . .
sight smell feel
. . . speckled *taste hear* laughter.

◆ ◆ ◆

BLUES

bp Nichol

144

JAPANESE MOVIES. 2

Sharon Thesen

He left her
to marry another woman
(rich, vain, ugly, stupid,
but rich) & advance his career
as a warrior-artiste,
but he missed her prettiness
her devoted love her long
long black hair.
Her form would appear to him
while he aimed at the target
etc., he would lose
himself in the vision.
Finally, after many years
he went back to find her
& he did, she was there
where he left her,
& just as beautiful as ever.
Her love too.
They slept together &
the next morning,
pure horror. She was dead
all skull & bones & dust
& her hair chased him
all around the rotting house
him yelling & terrified
& then with a soft, swishing
kind of sound it swept
down upon his neck &
throttled him
in his prime.

KITCHEN MURDER

Pat Lowther

Everything here's a weapon:
i pick up a meat fork,
imagine
plunging it in,
a heavy male
thrust

in two hands
i heft a stone-
ware plate, heavy
enough?

rummage the cupboards:
red pepper, rape-
seed oil, Drano

i'll wire myself
into a circuit:
the automatic perc,
the dishwater, the
socket above the sink

i'll smile an electric
eel smile:
whoever touches
me is dead.

BATTERED

Anne Marriott

(Peels off
  in onion layers from the purpled face
  innocence   hope
  exposes trust
  shrinking at the raw core)

She clings to doctor
when he shrugs away
the nearer rounded nurse
detached again
last chance the curved cold
white iron hospital bed
life preserver.
She sinks.

They loosen her fingers so gently one by one
the smallest still
in its tiny cast
from that earlier strange fall
pointing at dead ends
all around the room.

Parents
cry darling to the blotched face
through their bent lips
the blue bland surface of their eyes
drawn tight tighter
scarcely holding until they reach
the '67 Chev
where all the poison in their heads
can split the iris
spurt out stab
with hate hate hate
each other
each other's child
most of all that wretched child
each of them was.
That child.
Spat on.

Plastered finger tries
to scrape the spittle
stinging the broken bruise.

A COLOR

Cathy Ford

is red
specifically
> blood

red
> any blood

any red
blood is found in flowers
in the centre
red flows
> natural

''my water burst'' she said
''it was blood''

under the skin
> blood

red sacs hidden
> in fantasy costumes

bang
> red

blood red
stick a needle in
> and

red

the woman in the restaurant —
eat my fish and chips
with red
> ketchup —

watching
''is there a ladies in here''
> she asked

polite
> red blood

on her hands face
painted on her hands and face

"please" she said
"Get out," said the cook,
"You've been in a blood
                        bath."

he took her arm
                but
didn't touch the blood
                        red
redness

"Don't come back" said the cook
to the red blood woman
"You're covered in
                        blood."

let me take you home
i said
to the woman in red
i didn't want the coffee
                        anyway
the cook left
                blood red
red
        fingerprints
on the saucer
if
anyone
        drinks
                        red
out of a saucer
the cook says to leave
let me i said
to the red woman
blood woman
red blood skinned

TH AVERAGE CANADIAN NOSE BLEED

bill bissett

Sunday morning in Oakalla
pickin' off the crabs, tryin'
to break their backs, or

failin' that, drown 'em
in th overflowd sink, at
least can keep their numbers

down, rumor has it theres to be
a street movie shown today;
last nite on tv — burt lancaster

katherine hepburn in Th Rainmaker,
such a beautiful film, th message,
yu are what yu see yrself

to be, th ultimate in sentimental
solipsism, democracy, th faith
of our times, even J. Paul Getty
wud agree, etc., but hepburn
shows th truth of it, wud she becum
wholly human, that is, make it

with illusion, th camp of mid-west
pioneer nostalgia, etc., only th deluge
Starbuck promises cud possibly know

as th 10 pm curfew struck long befor
this really great etc. movie was ovr
nd the guards regretfully themselves

had to turn off th set, while th rest
of us were lockd in this lonely instance,
like, how do you spell realize

oakalla prison farm
jan/69

150

DOPPELGANGER

Peter Trower

You, the parallel me who shares this face
we have crossed shadows before —
I have sensed your prickly presence —
heard your insistent feet
preceding me or shuffling in my wake.

It began with voices saying:
''Man, you sure look like someone
I've seen before'' (but this is a common thing —
a simple case of mistaken identity) —
I thought it nothing until that first fat cop
calling me to a squad car, threatened me direly
as though I were some other duck-tailed punk entirely.

But I shrugged it off until the two dicks took me
up to the station to slug me under the lights
(it was in the days of the Mulligan regime
when the cops took payoffs and never used kid gloves)
growling: ''Okay, kid, we know you robbed that store!'' —
Struck five-years-old with fear, I stuttered my innocence
terrified they'd take me
into the elevator   halt between floors
and work me over until I confessed to murder
but a likelier call came in and they let me go.

After this, I began to get concerned —
Who was this shifty clown they had me pegged for?
I considered hunting him down for vague revenge
till I read of doppelgangers
those mirror-image omens of ghostly myth —
saw the doomed lovers meet their duplicate selves
in Rossetti's strange painting —
thought: ''What if he's mine? What if our confrontation
should trigger disaster?''
and I vowed to stay well clear of his crooked paths.

Yet it happened once more   my lookalike rolled a faggot
and they pulled me in on suspicion
(less-roughly since a recent investigation
had toppled the bad regime)
I sweated nevertheless
but the fluttery victim botched the identification
and they turned me loose.

Then it was many years and eventually
I began to run with a more-bohemian set —
I paid the price for my match-box marijuana
and at last, the ridiculous price for possessing it.

In the South Wing of Oakalla Prison
among meek-looking men who'd committed ultimate crimes
and murderous-looking men who'd written bad cheques
where the barred drums climb four tiers to the ceiling
and grisly things have been done beyond green doors,
someone nudged my side
saying: "Hiya, Jimmy, howinhell's she going?
Never heard that you'd been made."

I turned to a man I had never seen before —
a junkie Punch with a witch's quarter-moon smirk
who searched my eyes with the look of a long-lost brother —
who wore the scars of too much smack and disgrace
knowing he knew me   knowing   "Jesus, ain't you...?
Could have sworn you was Jimmy Dunworth. Sorry, bud."
The smile slipping like smoke from the hooked face,
he sloped off shaking his head.

So at last, I learned your name, my doppelganger —
you, the parallel me who shares this face
May we walk at crosspurposes always and never meet
in any unlucky alley this side of peace.

NOON NEWS

Brian Fawcett

reports a lone gunman on 3rd floor
4th & Fir, Vancouver
clear winter day, the air so clean
you can't taste it
                         The radio reports
from across the street & brought to us
by Money's Mushrooms sez the announcer
What Food These Morsels be
                                  while the police
move to the second floor, sweating by doorways
with the barrels of highpowered rifles
pressed against to cool their necks the gunman
holds a woman on the 3rd floor
he threatens to kill, she whimpers in fear

so that I'm caught between that image
of a woman about 40, blonde hair
& Shakespeare's dust rustling somewhere

Buses roll on Broadway, the News fades
& eventually all words shake loose
from the entanglement
to sharpen themselves against both time & events:

Eventually one man in critical condition, the woman
dead & the cops push the gunman into the back
of a black car & drive away

the News is brought to us
by Money's Mushrooms yeah

What Food These Mortals be

THE KOSYGIN DINNER

Helene Rosenthal

Which of these 500 women was invited on her own
account?   No matter, we have come/paired
with our men like so many attaché
cases.   "My indispensable wife,"   — so
The Minister of Public Works
professes
presiding at head table

— and all of us in the fond grip of public
importance, social dress.
Flattered with chablis, champagne,
rare golden sack.   (Takes me back
to Falstaff. But I'm wistful. Where we're at
is sort of black court comedy too   — lords & dames
a privileged press, subsumed
in a wide spread of trivia;
gulls in the rich wake of statesmanship —
spume
of Great Events)

                    — "The Queen!"
We scramble to rise   (Boorishly I
have vodka in my glass honouring Mother
Russia, but it's too late, we drink),   obediently
sit back, resume our strangers' discomfort
with one another and settle to tedium.
Speeches glide off tumescent
bellyfulls.   I suffer
sudden multiplied reproach in mine —
a thousand cuts
of beautiful B.C. murdered salmon!

and at least a cramp
of repression. . . the protest going on
outside the building   (an alliance
of ordinarily hostile-to-each-other
Jews and Slavs — nationalists, sub-
merged in a joint surge against Soviet ethnic
oppression.   It's the foment going on
that sours the stomach: the hatred.   Blood roused in slogan
and chanting against the ''Red Butcher'' of unknown
kin, loved only as victims, or that's
the impression.)

But a mighty fortress is Hotel Vancouver.
We are spared tidal testament
waves of emotion, inside   (com-
placent, unable) as he, ubiquitous
head of all this state — sad-faced
Alexei, Little Father,
his plump handsome daughter helping/ sweeten the taste
/of these political chores, good girl!)
— gets up to speak: intones
a hope
of shared technology, of hand-held peace.
While the ''security'' dragnet
plies invisible steel
from slits of surveillance,
sharp should the treacherous
shark of death surface in the gay
spray of the chandeliers, the fake
sunlight.

Pulled in these tides, our table
(made up of media-men mostly, and their wives)
lists awkwardly.   The men lean forward, keen,
sniffing sport.   The women slump, bored.
In the sea-sawing breeze,
only the waiters and waitresses move
with unconcerned ease, at home in their function.
They are the aristocrats
of the occasion.   We redundant ones
feed.   And soon it's clap   clap   clap
and at last it's over.
We begin to leave

some craning to get a closer look at the
Illustrious Guest   inside his fallible
armour of escorts.   He looks ill
or at least not looking
forward to leave.   As the wavering bubble of men
of which he is the vulnerable centre recedes,
his dread
of a sudden kill seems merely pathetic.
For it is we who are the real target
of this tired brutality
this undigested pretense
                                        — women trailing
the men, fed
and fawning upon an anxiety of power
not ours.

THE BUSINESS

Lionel Kearns

She wanted it all but
was too busy
having it
to get on
with the business
of getting it

He too wanted it all but
was too busy
getting on
with the business
of getting it
to have it

GASTOWN *during "urban renewal"*

Tom Wayman

Heavy smell of vomit. Urine.
Of clothes in which the sweat has dried
over and over, many times. Where the weave
is pulling apart. This on a few concrete streets
parking lots, back lanes. The Harbour Block.
Alhambra. Challenger Building. The Boulder.
Rooms stuffed with boxes of tin cans
for scrap. Piss Alley. Number One.

Twelve more cents for a bottle of wine.
Twenty-five cents. This is a stab wound
on the hand of a man in the wheelchair.
Police vans, waiting. Fluid
that is urine or beer or water.
Hey. Want to buy this?
Here is a thing that cannot stand
on its back on the asphalt. Something
face down by the bins in the alley.
The eyes of the woman who sells shaving lotion.
The man who drinks it.

Fluid on the bricks below the light pole:
blood, urine or wine. The cough that comes
out of the chest with black driblets of phlegm.
What is in garbage: newspapers, coat hangers, tins,
the slime of pickleseeds, jars. Food rinds. Rags.
Cigarette packages. Sticks. Eggshells. Glass.
What to look for in trash: copper wire for stripping;
bottles. The body. Marks on the face: bruises
like sharp jabs, and long, blood-skinned cuts. Blue flesh.

We are like angels here: our bodies
come here to work, eat in cafes with them
drink at The Europe. Angels afraid to hate God.
Hating the sinners. Laughing. Dreaming of torture.
We long to feel
one of our steel-toed boots
crush through the stubble of a face
drinking at a gutter.

We are angels.
Their life insults us.

ON THE JOB

Tom Osborne

IMAGE-NATION 15 (the lacquer house

Robin Blaser

the cloudy sky grows dark
the peacock jeers
the cuckoo disappears
the swans have gone

> the peregrine falcon, stately,
> sits in the bare cherry tree
> the radio says he really
> nests downtown on the roof
> of the Royal Centre tower
> but today he, stately, sits
> in the cherry tree
> the pigeons hide, the wrens
> fly away, the robins
> look for another garden
> this   *vocation for*
> *the invisible world*
> this second day
> he's visited
> even the cats get
> under the rhododendrons

the candlestick
from New Brunswick
is a clear glass cross
with Christ on it

it speaks French
or, rather, Pascal —
that wonderful note
he sewed in his coat —
''Certitude, Certitude,
Sentiment, Joie.
Paix''

after the fire in the lacquer house,
the point is transformation of the theme —
enjoinment and departure — like
the Christmas trees, stripped of all
adornment, burned on Locarno Beach,
January 8th, 1981 —
there were children in the catalpa
branches — one fell out into an
ambulance — his head full of wings,
oh, flower

(March 9, 1981, 5:00 a.m.

RESURRECTION IN VANCOUVER

Elizabeth Brewster

Sitting in Stanley Park
under a giant cedar
taller than any tree in Saskatoon,
looking out on all this Emily Carr greenness
and up to the gentle blue
of the sky beyond,
I am bathed in moist sunshine,
a soothing light,
and half wonder
if I might have died after all
on the train from the prairies
and been raised up again
in a Pacific Eden.

Surely that fat little boy
with a green balloon
is a remarkably solid cherub;
the young men with beards
are risen prophets,
and angels wander here and there
in long skirts or in slacks.

But I think
(watching the fountain playing)
if I had really died,
I should have enough friends here
so that at least one would materialize
lying sprawled under that willow tree
or come strolling down the path
to tell me the way to the rose garden
or where I could find the peacocks.

I can think of one or two spirits
who would probably suggest
a beer in the pavilion.

I remember my sister told me
of dreaming she had died
and was cruising through bland seas

toward an exclusive resort;
everything handsome and luxurious about her,
a lavish stateroom, decidedly first-class,
and people dancing on deck to exclusive music.

But the other passengers
all looked through her
as though she were not there;
she did not recognize a single soul;
and she sat in a deck chair weeping
all the way
into the harbour.

VANCOUVER POEM

Alden Nowlan   *For Elizabeth Brewster*

''Vancouver is an un-Canadian city,''
Betty had said, although probably
thinking about something quite different,
and I, thinking about something different,
had agreed — a conversation of no
importance except that afterwards
it came to us that it must have been the reason
the cabbie who'd driven us in from the airport
practically spat in our faces when we paid him:
he was an East Indian, and people
who looked vaguely like us
must have hurt him so badly that
he could mistake himself for
a mountain range or the Pacific Ocean.

SEA TREK ETC

Daphne Marlatt

   trickle of broken hose. old netting, sacking, rope.
paint everywhere. penboards on end & painted silver. poles with
bells to be fitted, new springs & line. the sound of a boat
rubbing against tire, whisper of rope, shift across rope as a
boat lifts or falls.

   Sea Trek, Elma K, Miss Nikko 70, ready,
day after day copper painted & caulked & overhauled, now they
wait, feeling that suck in green & oily shallows, feeling
afternoon leaf so close at hand, & late (derisive, clucking of
a gull domestic, finally) they wait, for headway out to the open
seas/ the open season, current, storm: & fish.

◆ ◆ ◆

FINN ROAD

Daphne Marlatt

''Seems like, with men around, you're always at the stove.''
Making cabbage rolls, something that keeps in a slow oven
when the boys come back, late, from fishing. It's her day off.
She sent to town to pay the bills, ''somebody's got to look after
that.'' But tomorrow she'll be up when the tide's full, at 3 or 4
in the morning, down to Finn Slough where her boat's moored.
Been out fishing for 20 years now. And walks, from counter to
stove, with a roll.

   It's a hot day, sultry, rain spit in the air.
There's cotton laid out on the kitchen table, a pattern.
''Making a housecoat,'' something cool to wear when it gets
humid. Seems like, whenever it's strawberry & haymaking
time, there's rain.

DEATH BY WATER

Robert Bringhurst

It was not his face nor any
other face Narcissus saw
in the water. It was the absence there
of faces. It was the deep clear
of the blue pool he kept on coming
back to, and that kept on coming
back to him as he went to it, shipping
out over it October after October
and every afternoon,
walking out of the land-locked summer,
out of the arms of his voice,
walking out of his words.

It was his eye, you might say,
that he saw there, or
the resonance of its color.
Better yet, say it was what
he listened for — the low
whisper of light along the water, not
the racket among the stones.

Li Po too. As we do — though
for the love of hearing
our voices, and for the fear of hearing
our speech in the voices of others come back
from the earth, we speak while we listen and look
down the long blue pools of air coming toward us and say
they make no sound, they
have no faces, they have one another's eyes.

TONIGHT MY BODY

Erin Mouré

Tonight my body
won't come home to me, it won't
hug me at all
It huddles naked three blocks away,
on the roof of the stone Chinese church
by a belltower
How its lungs howl out its anger,
its heart fizzes in the dark
rain!

Tonight I am faithless & wayward, I am
my cousin & my aunt
sitting on the shoulders of my body three blocks away,
both of them howling
fit to burst my ears, & me stupefied & cold.
My insides are smeared with warm sperm,
don't talk to me!
Tonight it's my body, I'm stuck with it, don't
talk to me, I'm finally out of the woods
& off the ferry-slip

over the Lion's Gate &
into Vancouver,
my skin lonely as a sail,
I've climbed up the wall of the Chinese church
& left my body angry there
When I cringe
it shudders three blocks away, I can't
comfort it, or coax it out
from under its relatives, to come nearer
to home,
& hear me, who cries for it-

FATHER/MOTHER HAIBUN 20
Fred Wah

I still don't know how to use the chopsticks as right or as
natural, bamboo fingers hands arms mind stomach, food
steaming off the dishes, rain or wet snow, windows, night
lights, small meals you'd grab between rushes (unlike me),
that's what you did, isn't it, went back to the cafe later,
on the nights we didn't have rice at home, me too, when
I first went to university in Vancouver I couldn't stand it,
I'd need rice, catch the Hastings bus to Chinatown, what
is it, this food business, this hovering over ourselves?

A little ginger, a little garlic, black beans, lo bok, Aunty
Ethel, the kitchen

SUMMER SOLSTICE

Brian Fawcett

Purple clouds at the horizon
laced with lavender the trees
blackened by the dusk the wind & sea
a dull roar.
                    The precision
of what I see doesn't compensate
for the precision of what is there to see.
they don't match up — like the hummingbird
I saw buzzing angrily
amongst the goldfinches this afternoon
there is a residue of frustration
& cruelty — the bumblebee I smashed
from the air thinking it a whitefaced hornet —
it thought my shirt
was a flower. Thus eventually
nuclear stalemate between the superpowers
derived from the concept of property
to mediate between poor perceptual reflexes
& the world. My neighbour
plants a red flag at the corner of his property
to make sure I can see
where these long weedy grasses end
& his mown lawn begins.

But the light, I have to remind myself
is not merely an aid to perception
which plus technical & social extensions of property
we've come to think of
as Intelligence — Light

has its own pleasures & I. . .
well, I took the bee from the grass
put it under the rosebush
their dark taught me
to see

IN WINTER

Jon Furberg

in winter in the yard,
Yes to the birds' waking cries,
even starlings, in the stern light
bare tree shrieks in a bare world

"We're in trouble," says Dad,
"we're in for it. What we need
is a good depression."

to wake and anger us, to see
what we are in the midst of —
more of less, for a change,
in our skins alone, finally,
in spite of higher wages
in logging camps, workcamps,
in dole lines shivering in almighty
cold, bankers in shoddy shoes,
no socks, brokers destitute,
coat collar against the wind,
like we were all in the same boat

In the fifties the siren
appeared in the schoolyard,
after the war: Eisenhower, Bennett,
Britain the greatest empire in
the world, pink all over the map
in the classroom. Where's Korea,
Mom? "In Asia." What's in the pot?
"Weiners and potatoes, in fact."

Here we are. In. For what?
for ever. Remember. Clouded over.

In the windowbox the rain
comes again to touch the roots
of untended flowers, thus,
and so they arrive, in ecstasy
come in by their necessity,
through a doorway, emerge in air
and breathe in — mere poverty,
shameless and shining

◆ ◆ ◆

THE TRUTH IS LAUGHTER

Robin Blaser

blindly visited
Vancouver street
high heels
and cherry trees
he leans forward
everyday,
brown eyes
sharp with delirium
at the corner
by Hudson's Bay
around his neck
the mystery and
the crucifix
the mystery
is tender
that's why
he likes it
we go
around him,
sparrows,
everyday

DOWN

Jon Furberg

down in history
through layers of bones,
shells of feasting, and also
rifle shells, casings from
heavy artillery — history
a succession of wars, their causes
and means, and the manner
of their ends — in bodies
twisted beyond number

but down on the street
two old men meet and embrace.
How excellent! their bodies
rocking in bent arms —
hats, canes, shoes askew
in a little jig of recognition,
gratitude, even love,
you've seen it, tough sinew
of legs rocking down
to knotted feet

down the street in peace
to the beer parlour,
down on nothing but luck,
essentials — enough cash
for more of what we need.

Food, drink, talk — it is
one another's company they keep
in passing: We must have
a long talk right now,
very long and lively.
old men drinking the evening
down, drinking down history.
And very old women
who still laugh

passing on. passing down.
the old warriors wink
and smile, then they cry
and don't know why,
but the ladies do, they know
why they cry, old flowers
along the wall wearing red hats
and so resemble poppies, sacred
flower of this day's lapel —
glasses full of amber emptied
down the holy tube

OCTOBER

George McWhirter

A spectacle.
The pyre of autumn paid for
each day in a single coin
of light. There is ambergris
to keep the cats
away from refuse and the green corpse
in the compost. In every place, the leaves
pile up — amber, purple and red.
Robins find no special place to die.
They are eaten up
by the ground.
I number the gardens, the fallen fruit
not eaten by householders who hoard
imported luxuries: camembert, Dom Perignon.
Against this neglect
work of any kind seems wrong.
There are two days
for burning in the city of Vancouver,
no days for harvesting the waste.

Wisdom is always a sensual regret; knowledge,
recollection of the first taste
of blackberry on the thumb.

In late September we visit the mainland
On the open-air deck
of the restaurant, a Japanese girl holds in her eyes
the mountains. Like petals, lobes on a blue lotus
they rise and ring the bay.
Still she recalls another place. Somewhere
in Morelos. A frog, a cockroach
and a worm. Through their skin
a conversation crawls. Pure
Mexican, German and a Finn,
indulging at the bar —
words, a woman and some gin —
a different taste for each species
to enjoy.
(How each thing loves the hate
and hates the love that opposition
brings.) Outside,
the moon crests white on dark.

Under the broken stalks of cane
in that southern place
the fields flicker browny black
with crickets.
As dry twigs to the fire that
consumes,
their legs sing out a siren song:

we are the wake of the cutters
who murder the stalk
with machete
in one motion. Lie down, weary man.

The crickets in the fields
with one motion of their legs
sing under the broken
stalks of cane; a few men
clearing, building a pyre.
The girl at the bar facing the mountain
tastes their ashes
still
on her breath.
Bueno, she says
when her companions offer her
a drink.

Opposite the Celtic Shipyard
on the Fraser River
a brace of Chinese women
wait for the truck to take
them home. They converse
not at all. With one motion
they feed their fingers
to the earth for carrots and cabbage
or they unhang the heavy tomato,
and their skin runs green
under the tap from the chlorophyl.

Good, these wet-backs waste
nothing. Through the light
behind my car
they slip
easy as earth
into a stream.

The mainland sinking
in the Strait as we travel home.

After the first heavy rain we stick
like suicidal seed indoors.

Pineapple suds
in the blender;
Omo suds
in the washer.
Indoors, they all
taste the same.

Goodbye, O. says,
motoring off to buy a bar
of chocolate and a cigar.
O hangdog Odysseus.
And at the door
stars clear your head
like wash of water
on a shore. Yet what matches the long
afternoons when you sail
on two lungs, a single flame
in your single skin. White
towards a patch of bracken,
a species
of blackberry, labelled
Himalayan. Your taste
for being grows
high
and accurate. A certain
taste for opposition
grows, for the dark
definitions of the sun.

KERRISDALE ELEGIES

George Bowering

Elegy Eight   *for Michael Ondaatje*

Today I saw two robins feeding on worms along Yew Street,
eyes wide,
              looking into the open air, they
were not beset by past and future and wishfulness.

All animals see with their eyes what is before them.

But we look elsewhere,
                          our eyes bind things
to our desires,
                  our fears mock the great trees
in this neighbourhood.

                          Oh oh, says the anxious reviewer,
this poet is not in control of his materials.

Only by watching the birds fly do we know
there is sky between the trees.

                          I force my daughter
to learn the names of the continents, names
that snare the past.
                      That's how we stay living
over centuries.

The robin sees me coming,

                                        his act
is not fear,
          he moves only to keep his eye on me.

He will eat and fly and die,
                              and reach eternity
without naming it.

                  We dissolve into hungers,
our breath disappears every minute,
                              we can measure
our remaining store with a hand-held calculator.

Not for a day do we live only in space,
where windflowers open without history.
                              We live on a wheel,
never in Sunyatta, where the lungs rest
un-numbered.

I see my daughter's body come to rest,
her eyes set somewhere I envy,
                         and like a miserly Latin master,
I wave my fingers before her face.
                    I'm afraid
she's visiting the domain of not-being,
not-bothering-to-be,
                    damn it, what a coward.
To sneer at the meditating cat,
                         to avoid the face
of the nearly dead,
                    who looks like an animal in peace.

We remember getting there while making love,
                                        nearly,
to losing all care,
              to the open,
                         where all that matters
falls away, nearly.
              Where only the other body
keeps us here.

              We come back finally
to looking at the watch on the familiar wrist,
reaching for the cigarette,
                         horizontal clichés,
                                        remembering
where the underwear is,
                    moving an awkward elbow
that keeps us from being nowhere.

                          The open had been
just beyond her,
               but you were in her, she
is after all,
        the world.

As I walk past the hedges of Kerrisdale all I see
is a translation of the open,
                     nature to our advantage
pressed,
       or the natural eye of a robin
looking past me to the sky.

                  Stupid fate,
to be nothing more than this,
                  a foreign timetable,
an unwanted designer trampling the woods.

Des forces que tu tiens ta liberté dispose,
Mais de tous tes conseils l'univers est absent.

If this hairy dog trotting down Yew Street
knew what I know,
                         he'd get my ass in his teeth
and never let go.
                         But he knows what his nose does,
and sees the first few feet of eternity.

                                          I know
the fiction of my past and expect to walk
straight into my fancied future.

                                    He walks,
we see indulgently,
                         on an angle,
                                    from bush to bush;
when we see a busy dog walk straight and quick,
we say how like a man.

Dog and robin,
                    we made no streets for you.

Yet look again at the dog's hanging head,
                                             a weight
we think we know lies on his neck.

                                    All memories
are sad,
          he has them too,
                              is this true?

We look
with whipped expectation for something
we used to curl up in,
turn in circles three times
and lie down.

It was tender.
We slept. Without
open eye we nuzzled and there we were.

Here
we have to run to reach,
but do we reach?

There — remember? — it was enough to breathe.
Home
was next to a loud heart.
Now we are in the street
too long for our feet.

Ah, those lucky little beings who never leave mother,
burrow in a womb that is world.
These curled
insects that live under the tatters of my gladiola,
fetal,
knowing all they touch was there
when they were born.

That happy robin again,
seems to know,
he may bounce or fly,
in a matrix
that includes the sky.

He does not know he is
the image of a pedestrian heart,
come from
a belly near another heart,
here to chatter between trees,
tipping wing,
skidding across his own wakened air,
like a pen across a modern poem.

Let us go then,
heart and eye,
to look as always,
attend as always,
look at the world and never
out of it.

It begins to fall down a little.
We renovate and proudly show our friends.

Cracks appear, and we patch them.
Cracks appear in us
and our friends appear to watch.
To be
watching.

Dogs walk by;
birds fly, away.

Why do I keep getting lost this way,
                              four blocks
from home,
               or is it a city away?
                              I get turned around,
no matter what street I take,
                         so I always look
like a man saying goodbye.

                              Like a banished citizen
allowed one last look at Kerrisdale,
                              yellow leaves
falling on lawns.
                 I hesitate,
                         trying to remember it all,
every day the same farewell.

Goodbye, warm world
who gave me birth
and told me
not to stick around.

I HAVE WALKED DOWN
INTO THIS CITY

Tom Osborne

I have, says Sonny
walked down into this city
without a dime in my pocket
and come out with the night
drunk and fed
   thirty dollars left. . .

I have figured it was no more go. . .
curtains, lead-filled overshoes
blood in the eyes
   a kid on the way. . .

I have been refused death
and service
beer and money
and sometimes love. . .
   a place to stay. . .

I have been given warm full days
round woolen nights
the soft curl of a lover's arm
   and the eight ball straight in. . .

I have never lived with the matadors
or the Arab tribes
the anaconda
or the tigers of Bengal. . .

never accepted the bad with dignity
or the good with content.
I have done nothing about famine
or slaughter — Expo '86 —
these leavings of the slipper
wicked sisters
pumpkins at midnight.

I have, it seems sometimes
not done much more
than walk down into this city
without a dime in my pocket
come out with the night
drunk and fed
    thirty dollars left.

SHUTTING DOWN FOR THE WEEKEND

Norm Sibum

On Saturday afternoons, wildly waving off customers,
the Hungarian shuts down his place for the weekend.
Sundays are for private life —
And to help, I drink the last of the coffee.
Like a wrestler mastering the art of the grotesque,
I unravel myself from a fall,
no longer invoking the names of American towns
that once might have come to my defense.
I stare into the faces of sentimental horrors,
bouncing them against the ropes.
But this street, with its love of weird Goliaths,
places no bets on shepherds like me.

I flip my mood like I would a two-bit piece,
wondering how it will land.
Heads or tails for the home-field advantage,
or blankly, without purpose, without anything to defend.
I lift my feet for the vacuum-cleaner
and the Hungarian jabs at the carpet beneath me.
Even the dust may harbor refugees —
He gets stingy with his unhealthy sanctuary.
I've become part of the rabble here.
But the moments I appreciate —
the repose that follows the thrill of mortal combat —
won't improve the chances of this shepherd's mild comeback.

And every Saturday mid-afternoon, a woman dines here
with her husband and devoted son.
By now she knows I'm attracted to her.
She occasionally looks my way,
sipping her wine with a withering tact only money
or harsh experience could have carved on her face.
She belittles nothing, praises nothing,
stoically drawing her family into conversation.
I should know better. I'm no Roman,
even if I meet her gaze like a gladiator
who lives from day to day — who can still move
but can't seem to recall the name of his god.

The Hungarian rattles his keys now —
'Wake up, chief. Let's go.'
His trivial pursuit of peace simplifies his existence.
The Sunday drinks will propel him
from his cradle to his grave,
while a more somber longing will tug at us
who still look for likeness in the flesh of another.
The snow that returns to the mountains
is a commitment that strips from the years
our worst memories. Again, we memorize the best.
All of us are waiting for beauty to bestow
its final meaning, its surrendering past.

◆ NOTES ON CONTRIBUTORS ◆

MILTON ACORN   The poet of Prince Edward Island, Acorn lived in Vancouver in the sixties. He is one of the founders of the *Georgia Straight*.

EARLE BIRNEY   This distinguished Canadian poet received his B.A. from the University of British Columbia and taught there for many years. He initiated a writers' workshop that by 1963 became the Creative Writing Department.

bill bissett   Although originally from Halifax, bissett's name has become synonymous with Vancouver. He is the publisher of blewointment press and has achieved a reputation as a visual artist and performance poet.

ROBIN BLASER   A key faculty member at Simon Fraser University, Blaser has had a profound influence in the community of Vancouver writers.

GEORGE BOWERING   A prolific writer who teaches in the English Department at S.F.U., Bowering can often be found watching baseball games at Nat Bailey Stadium.

BRIAN BRETT   Born and raised in Greater Vancouver, co-founder of Blackfish Press, Brett is also an accomplished potter, politician and gardener.

ELIZABETH BREWSTER   A poet and fiction writer who lives and teaches in Saskatoon, Brewster has written about Vancouver from a tourist's point of view.

ROBERT BRINGHURST   A poet, book designer and typographer, Bringhurst has lived for several years in Point Grey.

SKYROS BRUCE   Born in 1952 and raised in North Vancouver, Bruce was an accomplished poet as a teenager. Her name in the Squamish tongue of her mother is Kalala which means 'Butterfly'.

MICHAEL BULLOCK   A translater of books and plays from the French, German and Italian, Bullock has also exhibited his drawings and paintings widely.

BLISS CARMAN   Born in 1861 in Fredericton, New Brunswick, Carman was a poet of enormous reputation and influence in his era. He was Honourary President of the Vancouver Poetry Society from 1922 until his death in 1929.

BLAISE CENDRARS   Born Frederic Sauser in 1887 in La Chaux-de-Fonds, Switzerland, Cendrars fashioned a long and unique career in the annals of French literature. He alternated and combined travel and writing for more than fifty years.

STANLEY COOPERMAN   One of the most unusual and controversial members of the S.F.U. English Department, Cooperman created a completely distinctive literary style. He grew increasingly despondent during the seventies and eventually committed suicide.

JUDITH COPITHORNE   Born in Vancouver General Hospital in 1939, poet/illustrator Copithorne has lived in Kitsilano for the past sixteen years.

H. BROMLEY COLEMAN   Poet, playwright and actor, Coleman became a member of the Vancouver Poetry Society in 1917. He worked for the B.C. Telephone Co. and returned to England in 1928.

ANNIE C. DALTON   A major figure in the Vancouver Poetry Society, Dalton became the organization's second Honourary President and held this position for seven years. Her books were published in Canada as well as her native England. Born in 1865, she died in Vancouver in 1938.

BRIAN FAWCETT   In his student days at S.F.U., Fawcett founded *Iron*, a little magazine. In more recent years he has produced volumes of poetry and fiction, and worked as a community planner.

MONA FERTIG   Born in Vancouver in 1954, Fertig was the founder of the now-defunct Literary Storefront.

ERNEST P. FEWSTER   Born in England in 1868, Fewster moved to Vancouver with his family when he was twenty. He earned his M.D. in Chicago and set up medical practice in Vancouver in 1911. He founded the Vancouver Poetry Society in 1916.

MARYA FIAMENGO   Born in Vancouver of Serbo-Croatian heritage, Fiamengo, a resident of West Vancouver, teaches at the University of British Columbia.

CATHY FORD   One of the founders of Caitlin Press, Ford attended U.B.C. completing her M.F.A. in Creative Writing. She currently lives on Mayne Island.

JON FURBERG   A teacher at Vancouver City College, Furberg has been an important member of the zany group of characters that have been the collective force behind Pulp Press.

MAXINE GADD   A writer who first became prominent in the sixties, Gadd has remained an outspoken person and a poet of the neighbourhoods and the streets. She recently conducted poetry workshops at Vancouver's Carnegie Library.

GERRY GILBERT   A native of Calgary, Gilbert has exhibited, performed, screened videos and films and read poetry across Canada since the early sixties.

ELIZABETH GOURLAY   A resident of the city since 1950, Gourlay has degrees in library science from McGill University and creative writing from U.B.C.

DARYL HINE   Born in Burnaby, Hine's poetry first appeared in the fifties in Alan Crawley's *Contemporary Verse*. He has gone on to edit *Poetry (Chicago)* and resides in Illinois.

BETH JANKOLA   She fled a small prairie town for Vancouver in 1955, when she was nineteen. Jankola describes herself as "a non-aligned poet who has worked on her own for twenty years."

PAULINE JOHNSON   Born in 1861 on the Six Nations Reservation near Brantford, Ontario, she traveled widely and became celebrated in London by 1907. She was befriended by Theodore Watts-Dunton and Algernon Swinburne. Johnson settled in Vancouver in 1909 and celebrated the region in her poetry. On her death, in 1913, flags were hung at half mast and condolences poured in from all over the world. She was interred in Stanley Park.

LIONEL KEARNS   Born in Nelson, B.C., Kearns teaches at Simon Fraser University. He once played professional hockey in Mexico City.

JOY KOGAWA   Born in Vancouver in 1935, Kogawa, the daughter of an Anglican minister, is also a novelist. She and her family endured the humiliation, along with other Japanese-Canadians, of being interned and relocated during the last war.

TIM LANDER   A street poet and pamphleteer, Lander sells his broadsheets and tiny editions in bars, public markets, and wherever the tribes meet.

PATRICK LANE   Originally from Nelson, B.C., Lane lived in Vancouver for lengthy periods in the sixties and seventies. He is a founding editor of Very Stone House Press.

RED LANE   Richard Stanley "Red" Lane was born in Nelson, B.C. in 1936. Tragically he died in Vancouver on December 1, 1964 of a cerebral haemhorrhage.

DOROTHY LIVESAY   Few poets have stood the test of time as well as Livesay. Since her first published book in 1928, her writing career has flourished for over fifty years. She has been an integral force in Vancouver's writing community in every decade since the twenties.

MALCOLM LOWRY   Better known as a novelist, Lowry lived in the vicinity of Vancouver for seventeen years. His escapades and his cabin on the mud flats in Deep Cove have achieved for him the reputation of legend.

PAT LOWTHER   Born in Vancouver in 1935, Lowther grew up near the North Shore mountains. She was murdered in September, 1975, just at a time when her writing was beginning to receive national attention.

DAPHNE MARLATT   Born in Australia, Marlatt emigrated to Canada in 1951. She has lived in Vancouver since the early seventies.

ANNE MARRIOTT   A resident of North Vancouver for many years, Marriott, who has a national reputation, is perhaps one of the most underrated Canadian writers.

GEORGE MCWHIRTER   An expatriate Irishman born in Ulster, McWhirter came to Canada in 1966. He teaches creative writing at U.B.C.

JAMES MORTON   A poet of no particular reputation, Morton was writing about the bars and street people in Vancouver at the turn of the century while most of his contemporaries produced bad mock-Georgian verse.

ERIN MOURE   A member of the Vancouver Industrial Writer's Union, she has spent the past ten years working on trains.

E. ST. C. MUIR   Another obscure writer who appeared in eccentric private (undated) editions, Muir was at his best in documenting the plight of the ordinary man in the thirties.

JOHN NEWLOVE   Born in Regina in 1938, Newlove hitch-hiked west to Vancouver in the sixties and did much of his best work in downtown Vancouver.

bp NICHOL   Born in Vancouver in 1944, Nichol says he ''began concrete explorations in '63 after encounters with DADA & the writings of bill bissett. . . .''

ALDEN NOWLAN   A writer from New Brunswick, Nowlan came to Vancouver in the seventies and read with Elizabeth Brewster at Simon Fraser University.

TOM OSBORNE   Another member of the collective that founded Pulp Press, Osborne's political satire has appeared in various underground publications in Vancouver during the seventies and eighties.

AL PURDY One of the best known Canadian poets, Purdy was stationed in Vancouver during the Second World War. In addition, he worked in Vancouver as a union organizer and at a variety of jobs in the sixties.

A. RIPPON Rippon's work appeared in private undated pamphlets in the twenties. *The Indian's Prayer* is included as a piece of historical curiousity.

JOE ROSENBLATT Born and raised in Toronto, Rosenblatt is a visual artist as well as a poet. He came to Vancouver in the sixties and has been returning for lengthy visits ever since. Rosenblatt has written better than anyone about Stanley Park and the creatures that live there.

HELENE ROSENTHAL A graduate of U.B.C., Rosenthal has taught in Vancouver and at Malaspina College. In recent years she has turned her attention to studying music.

KAZUKO SHIRAISHI Born in Vancouver in 1931, Shiraishi was taken to Japan by her family just prior to World War II. She has an eminent reputation in Japan but is barely known in Canada.

NORM SIBUM A Vancouver bus driver, Sibum lives in the East End. His poetry has generally appeared in small limited editions.

JACK SPICER Born in Los Angeles in 1925, Spicer died in San Francisco in 1965. His long association with Robin Blaser brought him to lecture in Vancouver in 1965.

A.M. STEPHEN Born in Ontario in 1882, Stephen came west as a teenager and lived with his uncle in the interior. He was injured in his initial engagement overseas in W.W. I, leaving his right arm incapacitated for life. He taught school in Vancouver for many years, embarking on a political career in the thirties. Stephen was well known for his left wing sympathies. He died in 1942.

CLEMENT STONE One of Vancouver's earliest ''work'' poets, Stone wrote evocatively about the city's harbour and industrial areas of the thirties.

SHARON THESEN A graduate from Simon Fraser University, Thesen is the poetry editor for *The Capilano Review.*

PETER TROWER A resident of Gibsons, B.C., Trower has always maintained close contact with the underground elements of the Vancouver art scene. He can be found in residence at the Lamplighter Pub in Gastown nearly every Monday afternoon.

BURNETT A. WARD Dorothy Livesay remembers Ward by his nickname "Flare Pistol Pete". He was a member of the writers group that Livesay helped organize in 1936. They met on the beach at English Bay in an abandoned bath house.

FRED WAH A poet who has taught for many years in the Kootenays, Wah was one of the founding editors of *Tish* along with Frank Davey, Jamie Reid, George Bowering and David Dawson.

TOM WAYMAN Another member of the Vancouver Industrial Writer's Union, Wayman has been extremely active in writing and promoting "work poetry".

PHYLLIS WEBB Born in Victoria in 1927, Webb's thirty-year writing career has been combined with teaching and producing public affairs programs at the C.B.C. She currently lives in the Gulf Islands.

ALICE M. WINLOW The first Secretary of the Vancouver Poetry Society, Winlow was also a novelist, painter, playwright and professional musician.

GEORGE WOODCOCK No other Canadian has fashioned as varied a writing career as Woodcock. His work encompasses poetry, criticism, politics, radio drama, travel and biography. He remains one of the last of the breed — a man of letters.

◇ ACKNOWLEDGEMENTS ◇

Milton Acorn, from *I've Tasted My Blood*, The Ryerson Press © 1969, by permission of the author; Earle Birney, from *The Collected Poems of Earle Birney Vol. I & II*, used by permission of The Canadian Publishers, McClelland and Stewart Limited, Toronto; bill bissett, from *Nobody Owns the Earth*, House of Anansi © 1971, and from *Seagull On Yonge Street*, Talonbooks © 1983, by permission of the author; Robin Blaser, from *Syntax*, Talonbooks © 1983, by permission of the author; George Bowering, from *Kerrisdale Elegies*, The Coach House Press © 1984, by permission of the author; Brian Brett, from *Smoke Without Exit*, Sono Nis Press © 1984, by permission of the author; Elizabeth Brewster, from *Poems By Elizabeth Brewster*, Oberon Press © 1977, by permission of the author; Robert Bringhurst, from *The Beauty of the Weapons,* © 1982, used by permission of The Canadian Publishers, McClelland and Stewart Limited, Toronto; Skyros Bruce, © 1974, by permission of the Daylight Press; Michael Bullock, from *Contemporary Surrealist Prose*, Intermedia © 1979, by permission of the author; Bliss Carman, from *Bliss Carman's Poems*, McClelland and Stewart © 1929; Blaise Cendrars, from *Complete Postcards From The Americas, Blaise Cendrars*, University of California Press © 1976; Stanley Cooperman, from *The Owl Behind The Door*, McClelland and Stewart © 1968, and *Cannibals*, Oberon Press © 1972, by permission of Jennifer Svendson; Judith Copithorne, from *Arrangements*, Intermedia Press © 1973, by permission of the author; H. Bromley Coleman, from *One Morning*, Vancouver Poetry Society Chapbook, Number 1, Vancouver, © 1925; Annie C. Dalton, from *The Ear Trumpet*, Ryerson Press © 1926; Brian Fawcett, from *Creatures of State*, Talonbooks © 1977, by permission of the author; Mona Fertig, from *Releasing The Spirit*, Colophon Books © 1982, by permission of the author; Ernest P. Fewster, from *The Span*, Vancouver Poetry Society Chapbook, Number 1, Vancouver © 1925; Marya Fiamengo, from *The Quality Of Halves*, Klanak Press © 1958, by permission of the author; Cathy Ford, from *The Womb Rattles Its Pod*, Vehicle Press © 1981, by permission of the author; Jon Furberg, from *Prepositions (for Remembrance Day)*, Pulp Press, © 1982, by permission of the author; Maxine Gadd, from *Lost Language*, Coach House Press © 1982, by permission of the author; Gerry Gilbert, from *White Lunch*, The Periwinkle Press © 1964, by permission of the author; Elizabeth Gourlay, from *Motions Dreams & Aberrations,* Morriss Printing Co. © 1969, by permission of the author; Daryl Hine, from *Minutes*, Atheneum Publishers Limited, New York, © 1968; Beth Jankola © 1981, by the kind permission of the author; Pauline Johnson, from *Pauline Johnson: Her Life and Work*, Hodder & Stoughton Limited, Toronto © 1965; Lionel Kearns, from *Pointing*, The Ryerson Press © 1967, from *By The Light Of The Silvery McLune*, The Daylight Press © 1969, and from *Practicing Up To Be Human*, The Coach House Press © 1978, by permission of the author; Joy Kogawa, from *A Choice Of Dreams*, McClelland and Stewart © 1974, by permission of the author; Tim Lander, from *Gods*, Vancouver © 1975, by permission of the author; Patrick Lane, from *Beware The Months Of Fire*, House of Anansi © 1974, by permission of the author; Red Lane, from *Collected Poems Of Red Lane*, Very Stone House © 1968, by permission of Patrick Lane; Dorothy Livesay, from *The Collected Poems: (The Two Seasons)*, McGraw Hill, Ryerson © 1972, by permission of the author; Malcolm Lowry, from *Selected Poems of Malcolm Lowry* © 1962 by Margerie Lowry, by permission of City Lights Books; Pat Lowther, from *A Stone Diary*,

□□ INDEX □□